QUICK QUILTS

Compiled and Written by

Susan Ramey Wright

Quick Quilts
from the *For the Love of Quilting* series
Copyright ©1991 by Oxmoor House, Inc.
Book Division of Southern Progress Corporation
P.O. Box 2463
Birmingham, Alabama 35201

Library of Congress Number: 91-61188
ISBN: 0-8487-1053-3
Manufactured in the United States of America
First Printing 1991

Executive Editor: Nancy J. Fitzpatrick
Director of Manufacturing: Jerry Higdon
Art Director: Bob Nance
Copy Chief: Mary Jean Haddin

QUICK QUILTS

Editor: Susan Ramey Wright
Designer: Connie Formby
Senior Photographer: John O'Hagan
Photostylist: Katie Stoddard
Editorial Assistant: Lelia Gray Neil
Computer Artist: Karen L. Tindall
Assistant Copy Editor: Susan Smith Cheatham
Contributing Editor: Charlotte Hagood
Assistant Editor: Virginia A. Welch
Production Manager: Rick Litton
Associate Production Manager: Theresa L. Beste
Production Assistant: Pam Beasley Bullock
Additional Computer Art: Earl Freedle

To Mama.

C O N T E N T S

· · ·

Quick-Quilting Basics

Ilearned to quilt the way my mother quilts, the way my grandmother and her mother before her quilted—the traditional way: hand-piecing tops and hand-quilting them in a frame that sat on the floor. But the demands of a family and career severely limited my quilting time. So I was happy to discover rotary cutting, machine piecing, and other quick-quilting methods.

I've sacrificed nothing in quality for time saved. I've learned that a rotary-cut and machine-stitched quilt can be every bit as aesthetic, every bit as much a potential heirloom, as one that was cut with scissors and that contains nothing but hand stitches.

I still love and appreciate the old ways. In fact, I still prefer hand quilting over machine quilting. It relaxes me and lets me feel creative. But I know other quilters who enjoy hand piecing but prefer machine quilting, because the machine gives them beautiful results and allows them more time to piece by hand.

Not all the quilts in this book can be made in a day. Some quilts are quicker to complete than others. But with the equipment and techniques offered here, you'll be able to make more quilts in less time than your grandmother did and be just as proud of them as she was of hers.

The Rotary Rage

Perhaps you've already discovered rotary cutting. If not, there are a few tools you'll need to purchase. The **rotary cutter** comes in two sizes and several brands. The larger one is shown here. I prefer it because it allows better control, but I have used the smaller one with good results, too. You'll need a **cutting mat** to protect the blade and cutting surface. These also come in several sizes. I prefer a mat that is large enough to accommodate a folded width of fabric.

Finally, you'll need tools to measure your fabric and guide your cutter. I use a thick, clear, hard-plastic **quilter's ruler** to both measure and guide. Be sure the one you choose has ⅛" markings and a 45° angle. You may also find a **mini-ruler** handy for making smaller cuts, for extending your large ruler, and for use with your large ruler to straighten the edges of fabric.

Here are a few easy instructions for those of you who aren't experienced rotary-cutter users. The instructions are written for right-handed quilters only because I am right handed. If you are left handed, simply reverse the diagrams and switch references to left and right.

First you must create a straight-grain edge from which to work. Fold your fabric in half, aligning selvages. (See Diagram 1.) Place your quilter's ruler along the left cut edge, perpendicular to the folded edge and the selvages. Align your mini-ruler with the folded edge of the fabric. Slide the mini-ruler flush against the large ruler to straighten it. The large ruler is now aligned with the straight of the grain. Remove the small ruler. Holding the large ruler down with your left hand, cut all the way from the folded edge of the fabric to the selvages.

Now that you have established the straight of the grain, you are ready to cut a strip of fabric.

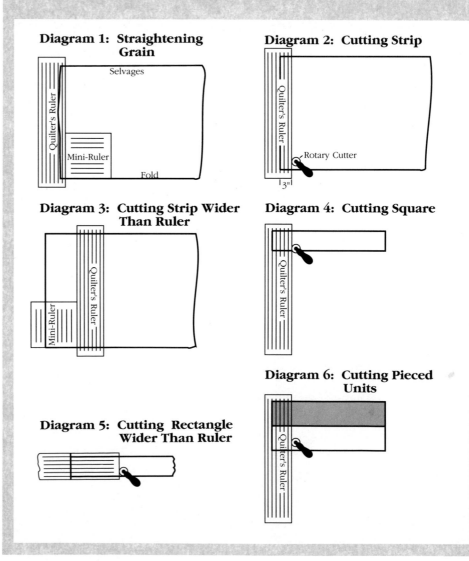

Diagram 1: Straightening Grain

Diagram 2: Cutting Strip

Diagram 3: Cutting Strip Wider Than Ruler

Diagram 4: Cutting Square

Diagram 5: Cutting Rectangle Wider Than Ruler

Diagram 6: Cutting Pieced Units

The squares, rectangles, triangles, and trapezoids in this book are all cut from strips. (*Note:* With the rotary cutter, you can cut up to four layers of fabric at a time.) First, follow the instructions to determine the width of the strip you need. Then with your ruler perpendicular to the folded edge of the fabric, place the mark for the measurement you need, 3" for instance, along the cut edge of the fabric. (See Diagram 2.) Hold the ruler in place and cut across the fabric. Should you need to cut a strip wider than your ruler, use your mini-ruler as shown in Diagram 3.

To cut a strip into squares or rectangles, place the desired measurement mark on the ruler along the short edge of the fabric strip and cut across the strip. (See Diagram 4.) When cutting a square or rectangle wider than your ruler, lay the ruler parallel to the strip and use the short edge as a cutting guide. (See Diagram 5.) Cut pieced units in the same manner as squares and rectangles. (See Diagram 6.)

Making Half-Square and Quarter-Square Triangles

Many of the quilts in this book use half-square and quarter-square triangles. To make half-square triangles, cut your square the finished measurement of 1 short side of the triangle plus ⅞". Using your quilter's ruler and rotary cutter, cut the square in half diagonally. To make quarter-square triangles, cut your square the finished measurement of the long side of the triangle (the side opposite the right angle) plus 1¼". Then cut the square into quarters diagonally. (Only right-angled triangles can be cut using these techniques.)

Final Word

Before choosing a quilt to make, be sure to read "Machine Quiltmaking" on pages 8–10. Other technique sections, "Stenciling Quilts" on page 38 and "Quick-Appliqué Techniques" on page 58, give you instructions for making the quilts in Chapters 2 and 3.

I hope you enjoy my special "quilt memory" stories on the first page of each chapter. These vignettes will tell you how and why quilts have become as much a part of my life as good books, good music, and good friends.

Happy quilting!

Susan Ramey Wright

CHAPTER ONE

. . .

It is July—a hot, barefoot July. Across the road from our house, wild primroses litter a bank with their party colors. Their heady scent hitches a ride on the transient summer air, riding as far as our long, shady front porch where Mama's quilting frame is set up. At the frame sit Mama and an elderly lady named Mrs. Patmon, a friend who often serves as our baby-sitter, my sister's and mine. Leisurely, but nimbly, their fingers work, taking dozens of stitches a minute through layers of calico print, cotton batting, and muslin backing.

Underneath the frame (four long beams supported by ladder-back chairs) my sister and I play out our childhood fantasies. We are cowboys, hiding here behind a mesquite bush from a war party of Cheyenne Indians. I am Tarzan and she is Jane, and this is our tree house, high above the African jungle. I am Cinderella and she is my fairy godmother, come to rescue me from the wicked stepsisters chattering above us. She will send me to the ball in a watermelon coach pulled by a team of barn cats and yard dogs.

The quilt, a scrap-bag profusion called Double Wedding Ring, will be finished before July has gone. It will adorn one of the beds in our house and warm us throughout the winter, now impossibly far away in the midsummer minds of childhood.

And for all the years to come, our memories of times shared in our playhouse world under Mama's quilting frame will come to us when bidden, to warm and comfort weary adult spirits.

SEWING MACHINE MAGIC

Your sewing machine can make quick work of the piecing process. And machine quilting can add a distinctive look all its own.

Machine Quiltmaking

The sewing machine is not new to quiltmaking. The machine has been used to make quilts ever since its invention in the mid-19th century. Many fine antique quilts can be found that are either machine-pieced, machine-quilted, or both. And combined with today's updated tools and techniques, your sewing machine can help you make more quilts in less time, keeping the quality and look you insist upon.

Diagram 2: Trimming Points

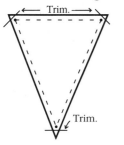

Diagram 3: Assembling Blocks

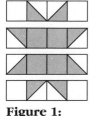 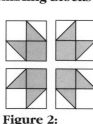

Figure 1: Assembling in rows   **Figure 2: Assembling in quarters**

Machine Piecing

Whether using templates or rotary-cutting equipment, be precise when cutting. Pieces that are cut off grain or the wrong size or shape, even slightly, will produce a pieced block that is the wrong shape and size and whose pieces don't fit together correctly or lie flat.

Another key to successful machine piecing is knowing where to set your needle to consistently attain a ¼″ seam. Unless your machine has a ¼″ mark, you will need to create one. To do this, set your needle so that the distance from the needle to the right edge of the presser foot is ¼″. Or measure from the needle to any point on the presser foot and mark that point with masking tape. Placing the ¼″ mark on the throat plate is not a good idea since the throat plate is often covered by fabric while you are sewing.

Set your machine for 12–16 stitches per inch. This creates tight enough stitches that backstitching is not usually necessary. Begin and end your seam with edges and intersecting seams aligned. This will be easier if you remember to press each seam as you go. I prefer seams pressed to one side (the darker side) so that the batting won't come through the seam. However, some quilters prefer seams to be pressed open since pressing to one side creates more bulk through which you must quilt. (See Diagram 1, Figures 1 and 2.) Make sure that intersecting seams are perfectly matched so that corners will match. (See Diagram 1, Figures 3 and 4.)

When joining two pieces with sharp angles, such as star points, it can be difficult to align the pieces accurately. First, mark corner dots on your fabric pieces. Then trim points to ¼″ from dots. (See Diagram 2.)

Many quilt blocks can be machine-pieced in rows or in quarters. (See Diagram 3, Figures 1 and 2.) Others are strip-pieced or quick-pieced in other ways. If possible, always piece in such a way as to eliminate the need for set-in seams, such as inside right angles or inside star points. However, if set-in piecing cannot be avoided, here's how to make it work: Stitch from one edge to the ¼″ seam line, stop, and backstitch. Remove your fabric from the machine. Align the remaining sides, backstitch, and stitch from the ¼″ seam line at the center to the outside edge.

Chain piecing saves time when joining several identical sets of pieces. Join the first two pieces. When finished, do not cut the thread but sew off the fabric for three or four stitches. Then feed the next two pieces through the machine. (See Diagram 4.) Continue until all sets have been joined. Then clip threads between sets.

Diagram 1: Aligning Seams

Figure 1: Seams pressed to one side

Figure 2: Seams pressed open

Figure 3: Intersecting seams aligned   **Figure 4: Intersecting seams not aligned**

Diagram 4: Chain Piecing

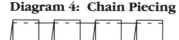

Sewing curves, whether by hand or machine, requires special care to ensure accuracy. Joining a convex (outward) curve to a concave (inward) curve can be tricky. (See *Pastel Fans*, page 14, and *Double Wedding Ring*, page 136.)

First, mark the centers of both the convex and concave curves. (See Diagram 5, Figure 1.) Stay-stitch just inside the seam allowances of both the convex and concave curves. Clip to the stitching on the concave curve. With right sides facing and raw edges aligned, pin the centers together. (See Figure 2.) Next pin the convex piece to the concave piece at the left edge. (See

Figure 3.) Carefully sew from the edge to the center, stopping frequently to check that raw edges are aligned. Stop at the center with your needle down. Raise the presser foot and pin the pieces together at the right edge. Sew from the center to the right edge, checking frequently to see that raw edges are aligned.

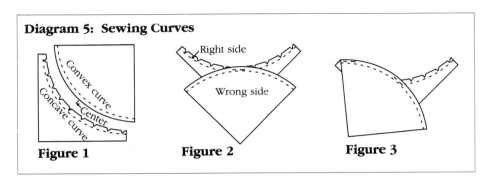

Diagram 5: Sewing Curves

Convex curve
Concave curve
Center

Figure 1

Right side
Wrong side

Figure 2

Figure 3

Machine Quilting

As the machine-quilted pieces in this book attest, machine quilting, in addition to saving time, adds a beauty all its own. Furthermore, it's sturdy and produces quilts that can withstand machine washing much better than can hand-quilted pieces. That can be an important factor with children's quilts and other items that will get a lot of use.

The backing and batting for a machine-quilted quilt should measure 4″ larger all around than the quilt top, because the quilting process pushes the quilt top fabric outward. After quilting, trim the backing and batting to match the quilt top.

Thread your bobbin with a good quality of cotton or cotton-covered polyester sewing thread in a color to match your backing. Use a top thread to match your quilt top. (Some machine quilters prefer to use a very fine invisible nylon thread on the quilt top. Invisible thread calls attention to the quilting outline rather than to the stitches themselves and gives the quilt a look similar to hand quilting.)

Straight-line quilting is perhaps the easiest form of machine quilting. If your quilt is to contain a combination of straight-line and free-motion quilting, do the straight-line quilting first.

On a flat surface, stack your backing, right side down; batting; and top, right side up. Secure layers with either thread or pin basting. (Some quilters prefer pin basting since basting thread tends to catch on the presser foot. If you choose pin basting, you will need, literally, hundreds of #1 or #2 safety pins—about 300 for a twin-size quilt and up to 600 or more for a king-size quilt. Place pins at 4″ intervals, avoiding lines where you will be quilting, if possible, so that you won't have to remove the pins as you quilt.)

Starting at one side, roll the quilt to the point at which the center row of quilting will be placed. Secure the roll with *bicycle clips*. (See Diagram 6.) These are metal bands that bicyclers use to hold their pants legs close around their ankles while riding, but they're great for holding a rolled quilt for machine quilting, too. Bicycle clips are available at bicycle shops and at some quilt shops.

Use an *evenfeed* or *walking foot* on your sewing machine. This presser foot is designed to feed the top layer of your quilt through the machine at the same speed that the feed dogs feed the bottom layer. Check with your sewing machine dealer if you don't already have an evenfeed foot.

Quilt from one edge of the quilt to the other, down the center. (See Diagram 6.) Then unroll the quilt to the next quilting line and quilt. It's a good idea, if possible, to stitch the first two rows in opposite directions to prevent the layers from shifting. Continue quilting, unrolling as you go, until you reach the edge. Then roll the quilt from the opposite side and quilt that side in the same manner.

For ease in handling, you may wish to quilt your blocks before joining them. (See *Heart's Desire,* page 70, for instructions on joining prequilted blocks.) If so, simply cut your backing and batting to match your blocks, layer for quilting, baste, and quilt. No rolling is necessary since you're working with much smaller units.

Diagram 6: Straight-Line Quilting

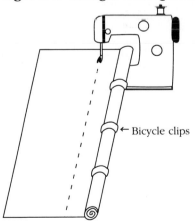

← Bicycle clips

Diagram 8: Mitered Borders

Side border strip (wrong side)

Quilt

Figure 1

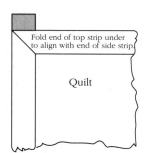

Top border strip (wrong side)

Quilt

Figure 2

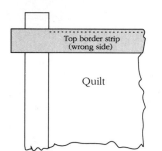

Fold end of top strip under to align with end of side strip.

Quilt

Figure 3

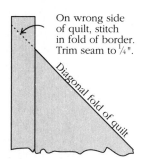

On wrong side of quilt, stitch in fold of border. Trim seam to ¼".

Diagonal fold of quilt

Figure 4

Press seam.

Quilt

Figure 5

Free-motion quilting allows you to quilt curved lines and fancy quilting patterns by machine. It can be used alone or in combination with straight-line quilting.

Replace your machine's presser foot with a *darning foot.* Drop the feed dogs so that you will be able to move the quilt in any direction—sewing forward, backward, sideways, or even in circles—without turning it. (If your feed dogs don't drop, you will need to use a throat plate cover. Check with your sewing machine dealer for a cover to fit your machine.) If you're a novice at free-motion quilting, an *embroidery hoop* is useful to keep the fabric flat and provide the right amount of fabric tension while quilting. (See Diagram 7.) Later, after you've gained experience, you'll be able to accomplish the same results with only your hands.

Diagram 7: Free-Motion Quilting

Remember, with the feed dogs down, you will be controlling the stitch length by how fast or slowly you move the quilt through the machine; the faster you move the quilt, the longer your stitches will be. Just as with hand quilting, you will want to make your stitches as even as possible.

Becoming proficient at machine quilting, especially free-motion quilting, takes practice, so don't become discouraged if it feels awkward to you at first. Layer some scrap fabric with batting and backing and practice quilting until your stitches are even and your lines go where you want them to go.

Making Borders

Because seams can vary slightly and some fabrics may stretch a bit due to type or bias cut, opposite sides of your finished quilt top may not be the same measurement. You can, and should, correct this when you add your borders. A quilt whose sides are uneven will probably hang crooked, whether displayed on a bed or hanging on the wall.

Measure the length of each side of the quilt prior to cutting the borders. Then, if opposite sides are not equal, cut two borders to match the *shorter* of the two opposite sides. Join the borders to the quilt, easing the longer side of the quilt to fit the border. Repeat with the remaining two opposite borders.

Mitered borders take some special care and planning. First, measure your quilt. Cut two border strips to fit the shorter of two opposite sides, plus the width of the border plus 2". Now center the measurement for the shorter side on one border strip and place a pin at each end of the measurement. Match the pins on the border strip to the corners of the *longer* side of the quilt. Join the border strip to the quilt, easing the quilt to fit between the pins, stopping ¼" from each corner of the quilt. (See Diagram 8, Figure 1.) Join the remaining cut strip to the opposite side of the quilt. Cut and join the remaining borders in the same manner. Press seams to one side. Follow remainder of Diagram 8 to miter corners.

Pieced borders take a little more time to make, but they can save a considerable amount of fabric. Unless otherwise indicated, yardage charts in this book allow for enough fabric for unpieced borders. But in most cases, pieced borders are fine. (Border prints usually do not lend themselves to piecing, since the pattern must be matched at the seams.) Refer to Diagram 9 to piece borders at an angle as follows: With right sides facing, lay one strip on top of the other to form an L. Stitch across the top strip as shown. Press seam to one side.

Diagram 9: Pieced Border Strip

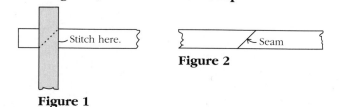

Stitch here.

Figure 1

Seam

Figure 2

Mexican Star

You may be surprised to learn that this magnificent quilt was pieced and quilted entirely by machine. And with your rotary cutting tools and the instructions that follow, you can make your own version without the use of templates.

Finished Sizes

Quilt: 83" x 98"
Blocks: 20 (12") Mexican Star Blocks

Fabrics

Navy print	4⅞ yards
White print	3½ yards
Navy pindot	1 yard
Blue pindot	½ yard
Backing	6 yards
Navy print for binding	⅞ yard

Instructions

1. Refer to Nine-Patch Construction diagram to make 9-patch squares as follows: Cut 5 (2"-wide) crosswise strips from navy print and 4 (2"-wide) crosswise strips from white print.

Join 2 navy print strips and 1 white print strip along long edges, alternating colors, as shown in Figure 1. Repeat with 2 more navy print strips and 1 more white print strip.

Join 2 white print strips and 1 navy print strip as shown in Figure 2.

Cut across 1 navy/white/navy band at 2" intervals to make 3-patch units as shown in Figure 3. Repeat with the remaining navy/white/navy band to make 40 (3-patch) units. Repeat with white/navy/white band to make 20 (3-patch) units.

Arrange 3 (3-patch) units as shown in Figure 4. Join units as shown in Figure 5. Repeat for a total of 20 (9-patch) squares. Set squares aside.

2. Refer to diagram for Cutting Trapezoid A to cut trapezoids as follows: Cut 12 (2"-wide) crosswise strips from navy pindot and 16 (2"-wide) crosswise strips from blue pindot.

With right sides facing and raw edges aligned, lay 1 navy strip on top of another. Measure 4⅝" from 1 end on *bottom* of strip and mark. (See Figure 1.) Place top of quilter's ruler at mark and 45° angle line of ruler along bottom edge of strip. (See Figure 2.) Cut angle as indicated in Figure 3 through both layers of fabric. This will give you 1 mirror-image set of trapezoids. Now measure 4⅝" from end on *top* of remaining strip. (See Figure 4.) Cut next set of trapezoids as indicated in Figure 4.

Repeat Step 2 to cut 56 mirror-image sets of trapezoids from navy pindot and 24 mirror-image sets of trapezoids from blue pindot.

3. To make B rectangles, cut 20 (2" x 26½") strips lengthwise from navy print. Cut across each strip at 6⅝" intervals to make a total of 80 (2" x 6⅝") rectangles.

4. To make C triangles, cut 40 (4¼") squares from white print. Cut squares into quarters diagonally to make 160 quarter-square triangles. (See Making Half-Square and Quarter-Square Triangles, page 5.)

5. To make D triangles, cut 40 (4⅝") squares from white print. Cut squares in half diagonally to make 80 half-square triangles.

6. Follow Block Assembly diagram on page 13 to make 20 Mexican Star blocks. Trim corners of B pieces even with edges of block as shown in Block Assembly diagram.

7. To make pieced sashing squares, cut 7 (4¼") squares from navy print and 7 (4¼") squares from white print. Cut squares into quarters diagonally to make 28 navy print quarter-square

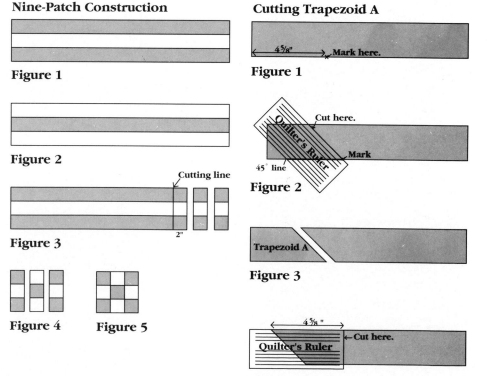

Nine-Patch Construction

Figure 1

Figure 2

Cutting line

2"

Figure 3

Figure 4   **Figure 5**

Cutting Trapezoid A

4⅝" Mark here.

Figure 1

Cut here.

Quilter's Ruler

Mark

45° line

Figure 2

Trapezoid A

Figure 3

4⅝"

Cut here.

Quilter's Ruler

Figure 4

triangles and 28 white print quarter-square triangles.

Join 1 navy print quarter-square triangle and 1 white print quarter-square triangle. Repeat. Then join to form square. (See pieced sashing squares in Quilt Top Assembly diagram.) Repeat for a total of 14 navy/white pieced sashing squares.

To make unpieced sashing squares, cut 4 (3½″) squares from navy print and 12 (3½″) squares from white print.

Cut 18 (3½″ x 12½″) sashing strips from navy print and 31 (3½″ x 12½″) sashing strips from white print.

8. Follow Quilt Top Assembly diagram to join Mexican Star blocks with sashing strips, pieced squares, and un-pieced squares.

9. Cut 2 (10½″-wide) borders from navy print and join to top and bottom of quilt. Cut 2 (10½″-wide) borders from navy print and join to sides of quilt.

10. Machine-quilt, following piecing lines. (See Machine Quilting, page 9.) Bind with navy print.

Quilt Top Assembly

Block Assembly

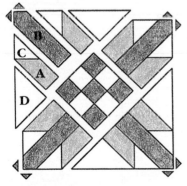

Finished Block

Sugar and Spice and Patchwork Nice

Soft prints and satin ribbons combine in these girlish versions of two traditional quilt designs to add warmth to a little girl's room. Two layers of high-loft batting give them a comforter look and feel. And machine piecing and hand tying make them easy and quick to stitch.

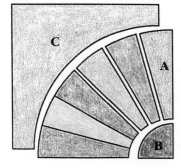

PASTEL FANS

Finished Sizes
Quilt: 75" x 96"
Blocks: 48 (10½") Fan Blocks

Fabrics and Materials
Assorted pastel prints	6¾ yards
Inner border	2½ yards
Outer border	2¾ yards
Backing	5⅞ yards

21 yards (¼"-wide) satin ribbon in assorted pastels
Yarn needle

Instructions
1. Cut pieces as indicated on templates on pages 16 and 17.
2. Follow Block Assembly diagram to machine-piece 48 blocks. (See page 8 for instructions for sewing curves.)

Block Assembly

3. Follow Quilt Top Assembly diagram to join blocks in 8 horizontal rows of 6 blocks each.

4. Cut 2 (3½″-wide) inner borders and join to sides of quilt. Cut 2 (3½″-wide) inner borders and join to top and bottom of quilt.

5. Cut 2 (3½″-wide) outer borders and join to sides of quilt. Cut 2 (3½″-wide) outer borders and join to top and bottom of quilt.

6. Layer batting; top, right side up; and backing, right side down. With batting against feed dogs, join layers along sides and bottom. Turn through opening. Slipstitch opening closed.

7. Cut ribbon into 63 (12″) pieces. Beginning at center of quilt, tie bows at all block corners as follows: Thread yarn needle with 1 (12″) length of ribbon. Sew ribbon through all layers and tie bow on top. (Bows can be secured with matching thread if desired.) Machine-quilt in-the-ditch between inner and outer borders.

Quilt Top Assembly

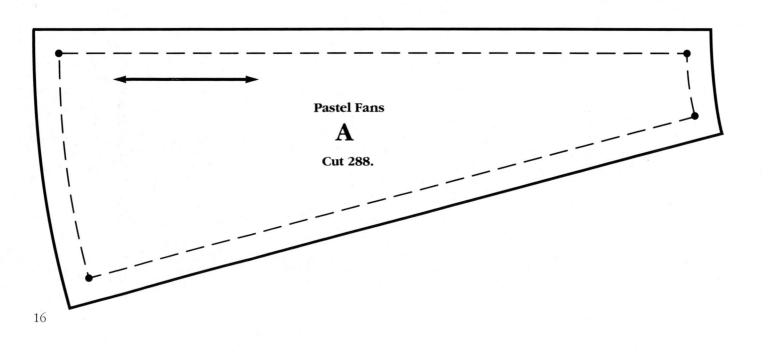

Pastel Fans

A

Cut 288.

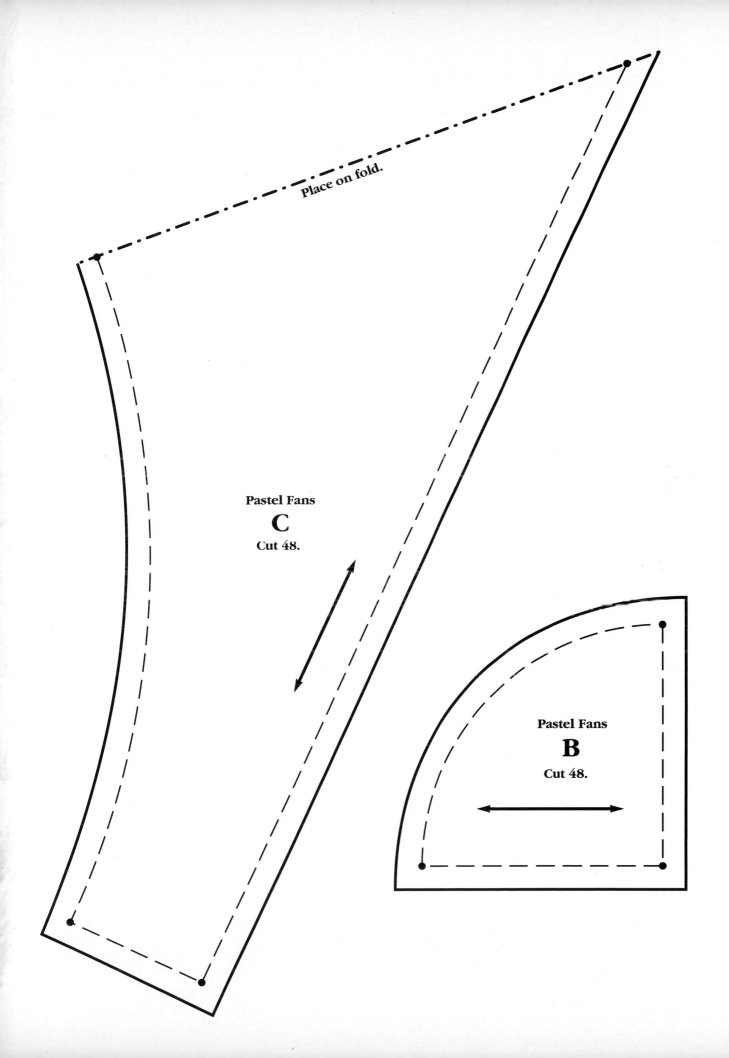

Place on fold.

Pastel Fans
C
Cut 48.

Pastel Fans
B
Cut 48.

17

LOG CABIN PARFAIT

Finished Sizes
Quilt: 75" x 96"
Blocks: 48 (10½") Log Cabin Blocks

Fabrics and Materials
Assorted prints and solids	6 yards
Inner border	2½ yards
Outer border	2¾ yards
Backing	5⅞ yards

21 yards (¼"-wide) satin ribbon in assorted colors
Yarn needle

Instructions

1. Cut 48 (2") center squares from assorted prints and solids. Cut remaining fabric into 2"-wide strips.

2. Refer to Block Assembly diagram to machine-piece 48 blocks as follows: With right sides facing and raw edges aligned, join a 2"-wide strip to a center square. Trim strip to match length of center square. (See Figure 1.) Fold strip out and finger-press seam.

3. Working clockwise around center of the block, add a second strip, aligning edges and stitching across width of center square and first strip. Trim strip to match width of center square and first strip. (See Figure 2.) Fold strip out and finger-press seam.

4. Add a third strip as shown in Figure 3. Continue adding strips clockwise to complete block. (See Log Cabin Block diagram for finished block.)

5. Follow Steps 3–7 of instructions for *Pastel Fans,* page 16.

Block Assembly

Center square
Strip 1

Figure 1

Center square
Strip 1
Strip 2

Figure 2

Center square
Strip 1
Strip 3
Strip 2

Figure 3

Quilt Top Assembly

Log Cabin Block

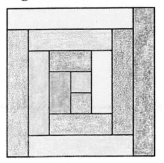

Tucked Muslin Pillow

Quilted hearts and tucked borders on creamy muslin add a touch of romance to this pillow, which is pieced in a variation of the Log Cabin block.

Finished Size
Pillow: 17½" (excluding ruffle)

Fabrics and Materials
Muslin   2 yards
Batting   19" square
Water-soluble pen
Polyester stuffing or 17½" pillow
   form

Instructions
1. From muslin, cut 1 (6½")
square; 1 (19") square; 1 (18") square;
2 (2" x 42") strips; 2 (6½" x 12½")
strips; 2 (6½" x 18") strips; and 2 (8" x
67") strips.

2. Center and transfer Heart Quilting Pattern below to right side of 6½"
muslin square.

3. Layer 19" square, right side
down; batting; and 6½" square, right
side up and centered on batting. Baste
through all layers.

4. Machine-quilt hearts.

5. Beginning at top of center heart
square and using 2" x 42" strips, build
block in log cabin fashion as follows:
With right sides facing and raw edges
aligned, lay strip on top of heart
square with end of strip at 1 edge of
the square. Machine-stitch through all
layers to join. Trim strip even

with square. Fold strip out and finger-
press seam. Referring to Pillow Assembly diagram on page 21 and working
clockwise around square, add a second strip, aligning edges and stitching
down length of square and first strip.
Trim strip to match length of square
and first strip. Fold strip out and
finger-press.

Continue adding strips clockwise
around square until you have joined 8
strips in order indicated on Pillow Assembly diagram. (If you aren't familiar
with this form of log cabin piecing,
refer to Block Assembly diagram on
page 18.) Trim backing and batting
even with top of block.

6. Starting ¾" from long edge of 1
(6½" x 12½") strip, use water-soluble
pen to mark 14 stitching lines down
length of strip. (See Making Tucks, Figure 1.) Fold, matching stitching lines
as shown in Figure 1. Stitch tucks.
Press tucks toward top of strip. (See
Figure 2.)

7. Refer to Pillow Assembly diagram and photograph. Starting 1¾"
from left end of strip, turn tucks toward bottom of strip (against the direction in which tucks are pressed)
and stitch from top to bottom across
all tucks. Measure 1½" from this stitching line and stitch from bottom to top
across all tucks (in the direction in
which the tucks are pressed). Continue stitching across tucks in opposite directions at 1½" intervals across
length of strip. Repeat Steps 6 and 7
for remaining 6½" x 12½" strip and
for both 6½" x 18" strips.

8. Follow Pillow Assembly diagram
to join tucked strips to block.

9. To make ruffle, join 8" x 67"
strips at ends to form 8" x 134" strip.
Join ends to form continuous strip.
With wrong sides facing and raw
edges aligned, fold strip in half lengthwise and press. Gather raw edge to fit
perimeter of pillow top. With raw
edges aligned, baste ruffle to right
side of pillow top.

10. With right sides facing, raw
edges aligned, and ruffle on inside,
join pillow back (18" square) to pillow
top along 3 sides. Clip corners and
turn pillow. Fill with stuffing or insert
pillow form. Slipstitch opening closed.

Heart Quilting Pattern

Pillow Assembly

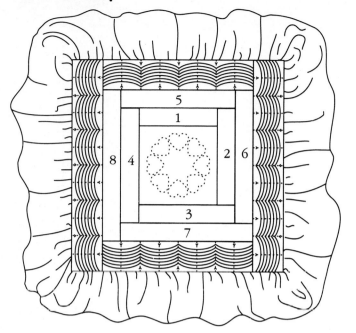

Making Tucks

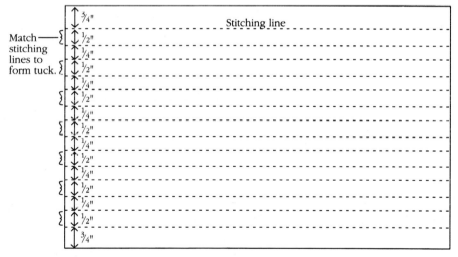

Figure 1

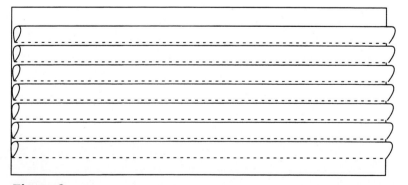

Figure 2

Roman Candle

This fiery red variation of the Roman Stripes design was hand-pieced and quilted many years ago. With rotary-cutting tools and the strip-piecing instructions that follow, you can beat that quilter's time by weeks.

Finished Sizes
Quilt: 69″ x 89″
Blocks: 48 (10″) Blocks

Fabrics

Assorted red prints	2½ yards
Assorted red solids	2½ yards
Red print border	2½ yards
Red solid border	2½ yards
Backing	5½ yards

Instructions

1. Refer to Block Construction diagram to make 48 blocks as follows: Cut assorted red prints and solids into 3″-wide strips. Join 1 print strip and 1 solid strip as shown in Figure 1. Press seam toward darker fabric. Cut across pieced strip at 5½″ intervals as shown in Figure 2. Repeat above procedure to make 192 (2-patch) units.

2. Join 4 (2-patch) units, pinwheel style, with solid red rectangles in middle of block as shown in Figure 3. Continue to join 2-patch units to make 48 blocks.

3. Follow Quilt Top Assembly diagram to join blocks in 8 horizontal rows of 6 blocks each. Join rows.

4. Cut 2 (2″-wide) inner borders from red print and join to sides of quilt. Cut 2 (3½″-wide) outer borders from red solid and join to sides of quilt.

5. Cut 2 (2″-wide) inner borders from red print and join to top and bottom of quilt. Cut 2 (3½″-wide) outer borders from red solid and join to top and bottom of quilt.

6. Prepare backing to extend 2¼″ beyond edges of quilt top. Outline-quilt all pieces by machine or hand, as desired. Fold backing to front of quilt to form 1″ self binding, turn under raw edge ¼″, and slipstitch.

Block Construction

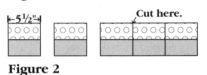

Figure 1

|←—5½″—→| ... Cut here.

Figure 2

Figure 3

Quilt Top Assembly

You can make a reproduction of this antique quilt without using a template, following the easy strip-piecing method outlined above.

Flying Geese

The triangles that make up the Flying Geese blocks are a snap to rotary-cut and machine-piece. This quilt is just right for a twin-size bed or daybed or as a sofa quilt. But it's easy to increase this design to any size you wish simply by adding more geese to the bottom of each strip for length and more finished geese strips and sashing strips for width. Sashing and border widths can also vary, depending on your choice of fabric.

Vertical bands of Flying Geese blocks, joined by bands of border print, combine in this quilt design that's easy enough for a beginner.

Finished Sizes
Quilt: 51½″ x 65″
Blocks: 174 (2″ x 4½″) Geese Blocks

Fabrics
Assorted dk. prints   1⅜ yards
Assorted lt. prints   1⅝ yards
Border print   2 yards*
Backing   4 yards

*The print in your border print will dictate the width of your borders. You might need more yardage for borders and sashing that are wider than 3½″.

Instructions

1. To make triangle A, cut 7 (6¼″-wide) crosswise strips from dk. prints. Cut strips into 6¼″ squares. Cut squares into quarters diagonally to make 174 quarter-square triangles.

(See Making Half-Square and Quarter-Square Triangles, page 5.)

2. To make triangle B, cut 15 (3⅜″-wide) crosswise strips from lt. prints. Cut strips into 3⅜″ squares. Cut squares in half diagonally to make 348 half-square triangles.

3. Refer to Block Assembly diagram to make blocks as follows: With right sides facing and raw edges aligned, join base of 1 B triangle to left side of A triangle, stitching from edge to edge, as shown in Figure 1. Finger-press seam toward B. (See Figure 2.) With right sides facing and raw edges aligned, join base of second B triangle (made of same print as first B triangle) to right side of A triangle, stitching

from edge to edge, as shown in Figure 3. Trim seam extensions even with block as shown in Figure 4. Repeat Step 3 to make 174 blocks.

4. Join 29 blocks to form 1 vertical row. Repeat to make 6 vertical rows. Cut 5 sashing strips from border print the length of rows. Join vertical rows with border print sashing strips as shown in photograph and Quilt Top Assembly diagram.

Cut 4 strips from border print and join to sides of quilt, mitering corners.

5. Quilt blocks as shown in Quilting Diagram. Follow print in fabric to quilt sashing and border strips.

6. Bind with bias binding or turn backing to front to form self binding.

Block Assembly

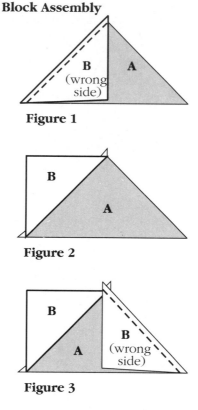

Figure 1

Figure 2

Figure 3

Figure 4

Quilting Diagram

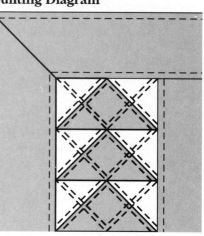

Quilt Top Assembly

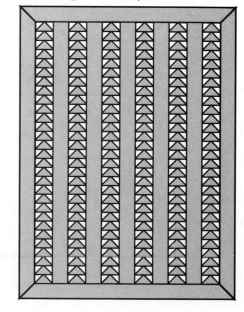

Attic Windows

This design is an excellent
choice for a scrap-quilt project.
For best results, choose a very dark
solid for the square. Try more than
one dark solid if you're adventurous.
Then divide your print scraps into
two categories: dark and light.

Finished Sizes
Quilt: 84" x 109"
Blocks: 266 (5") Window Blocks

Fabrics
Dk. solid	1½ yards
Assorted dk. prints	4½ yards
Assorted lt. prints	4½ yards
Inner border	⅜ yard
Outer border	1½ yards
Backing	6¼ yards
Dk. solid for binding	1 yard

Instructions

1. Cut 266 squares from dk. solid as follows: Cut fabric into 17 (2½"-wide) crosswise strips. Cut strips into 2½" squares. (*Note:* Strips may be stacked so that several layers can be cut at a time.)

2. To cut trapezoids, cut assorted dk. and lt. prints into 3½"-wide crosswise strips. (If you are using scrap-bag fabric, the length of strips may vary. Therefore, you will need to cut as many strips as necessary to yield 266 trapezoids from dk. print and 266 trapezoids from lt. print.)

Quilt Top Assembly

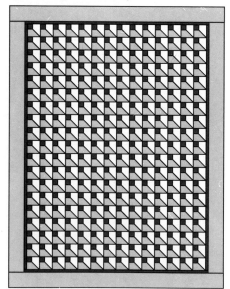

With right sides facing and raw edges aligned, lay 1 lt. print strip on top of 1 dk. print strip. Refer to diagram for Cutting Trapezoid A on page 12, substituting 5⅞" for measurement on diagram. Measure 5⅞" from 1 end on bottom of strip and mark. Place top of quilter's ruler at mark and 45° angle line of ruler along *bottom* edge of strip as shown in Figure 2 of diagram. Cut angle as indicated through both layers of fabric. This will give you 1 mirror-image set of trapezoids. (See Figure 3.)

Measure 5⅞" from cut end on *top* of remaining strip as shown in Figure 4. Cut next set of trapezoids as indicated. Repeat Step 2 to cut 266 mirror-image sets of trapezoids.

3. Follow Block Assembly diagram to make block as follows: Join 1 side of square to short side of lt. print trapezoid, starting at outside edge, stopping at ¼" seam line, and backstitching. (See Figure 1.) Press seam toward square. Next, join short side of dk. print trapezoid to square, starting at outside edge, stopping where previous seam begins, and backstitching. (See Figure 2.) Finally, with right sides facing and raw edges aligned, join trapezoids along diagonal sides, stitching from outside edge to seam at square. Backstitch. (See Figure 3.)

Repeat Step 3 to make 266 blocks.

4. Following photograph and Quilt Top Assembly diagram, join blocks in 19 horizontal rows of 14 blocks each. Join rows.

5. To make narrow inner borders, cut 9 (½"-wide) crosswise strips. Piece as necessary to make borders and join to quilt as shown in Quilt Top Assembly diagram.

6. To make wide outer borders, cut 9 (6½"-wide) crosswise strips. Piece as necessary to make borders and join to quilt as shown.

7. Quilt blocks in-the-ditch. Quilt outer border with diagonal lines (see photograph).

8. Bind with bias binding (see Binding Your Quilt, page 89) made from dk. solid.

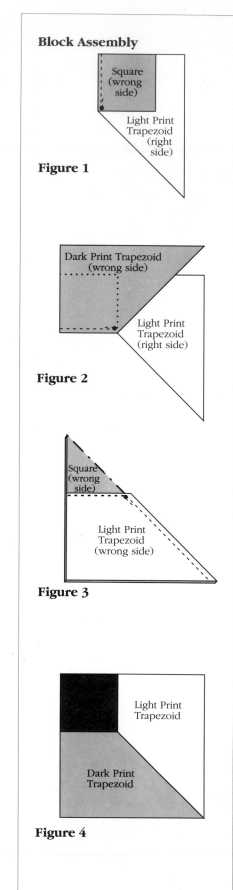

Block Assembly

Figure 1

Figure 2

Figure 3

Figure 4

Fabrics

Dk. rose print	¾ yard
Med. rose print	¾ yard
Med. blue print	¾ yard
Lt. print	¾ yard
Dk. blue print	1¼ yards
Lt. rose print	1¼ yards
Lt. blue solid for inner border	2½ yards
Rose solid for outer border	2⅝ yards
Backing	5¼ yards
Rose solid for binding	⅞ yard

Buckeye Beauty

Careful placement of light and dark fabrics makes this quilt classic appear to be pieced in a series of diagonal stripes. But the easy techniques for quick piecing and assembling described below will help you unravel the mysteries of its simple four-patch design.

Instructions

1. Refer to Four-Patch Construction diagram to make 45 Block As from dk. rose print and med. rose print as follows: Cut 7 (3"-wide) crosswise strips from each fabric. With right sides facing and raw edges aligned, join 1 dk. rose fabric strip to 1 med. rose fabric strip along 1 long edge. Press seam toward darker fabric. Cut across pieced strip at 3" intervals as shown in Figure 1. Join and cut remaining strips in this manner to make 90 (2-color) units.

Join 2 (2-color) units to form block as shown in Figure 2. Continue joining 2-color units in chain-piecing fashion until all units are joined. (See page 8 for chain-piecing instructions.) Cut blocks apart and press seams.

Repeat above step to make 45 Block Bs from med. blue print and lt. print.

Four-Patch Construction

Cut here.   3"

Figure 1

Figure 2

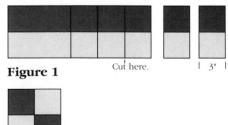

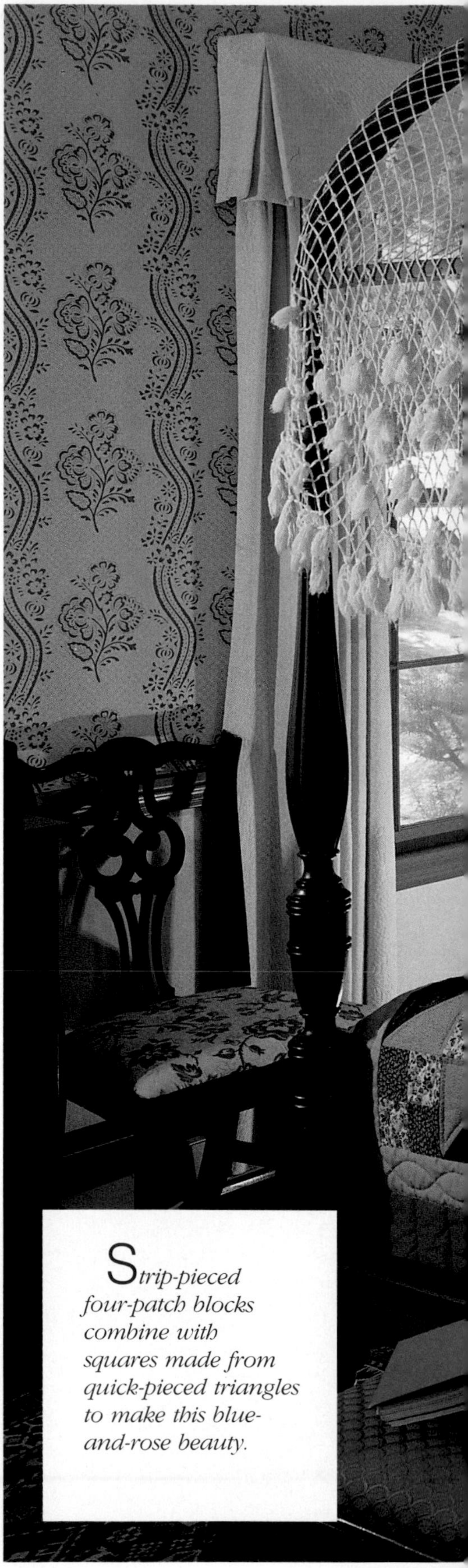

Strip-pieced four-patch blocks combine with squares made from quick-pieced triangles to make this blue-and-rose beauty.

2. Referring to Quick-Piece Triangle Method diagram, make 90 Block Cs from dk. blue print and lt. rose print as follows: With right sides facing and raw edges aligned, lay 1 fabric on top of the other. Use Quick-Piece Triangle Template on page 34 to trace 90 triangles onto fabric in manner shown in Figure 1. Machine-stitch ¼" on either side of drawn diagonal lines (see Figure 2). Cut apart along drawn horizontal and vertical lines (see Figure 3) to form 2-layer squares. Cut squares apart along drawn diagonal lines between lines of stitching to form 2-layer triangles (see Figures 4 and 5). Unfold triangles and press seam toward darker fabric to form Block Cs (see Figure 6).

3. Follow Quilt Top Assemby diagram to join blocks in 15 horizontal rows of 12 blocks each. Join rows.

4. Cut 4 (3"-wide) inner borders and join to quilt, mitering corners.

5. Cut 4 (4"-wide) outer borders and join to quilt, mitering corners.

6. Quilt as shown in photograph, using quilting patterns on pages 34 and 35.

7. Make continuous bias binding and bind quilt (see page 89).

Quick-Piece Triangle Method

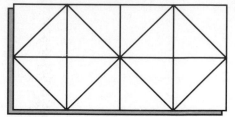

Figure 1

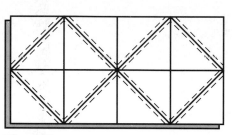

Figure 2

Figure 3

Figure 4

Figure 5

Figure 6

Quilt Top Assembly

A	C	B	C rev	A	C	B	C rev	A	C	B	C rev
C	B	C rev	A	C	B	C rev	A	C	B	C rev	A
B	C rev	A	C	B	C rev	A	C	B	C rev	A	C
C rev	A	C	B	C rev	A	C	B	C rev	A	C	B
A	C	B	C rev	A	C	B	C rev	A	C	B	C rev
C	B	C rev	A	C	B	C rev	A	C	B	C rev	A
B	C rev	A	C	B	C rev	A	C	B	C rev	A	C
C rev	A	C	B	C rev	A	C	B	C rev	A	C	B
A	C	B	C rev	A	C	B	C rev	A	C	B	C rev
C	B	C rev	A	C	B	C rev	A	C	B	C rev	A
B	C rev	A	C	B	C rev	A	C	B	C rev	A	C
C rev	A	C	B	C rev	A	C	B	C rev	A	C	B
A	C	B	C rev	A	C	B	C rev	A	C	B	C rev
C	B	C rev	A	C	B	C rev	A	C	B	C rev	A
B	C rev	A	C	B	C rev	A	C	B	C rev	A	C

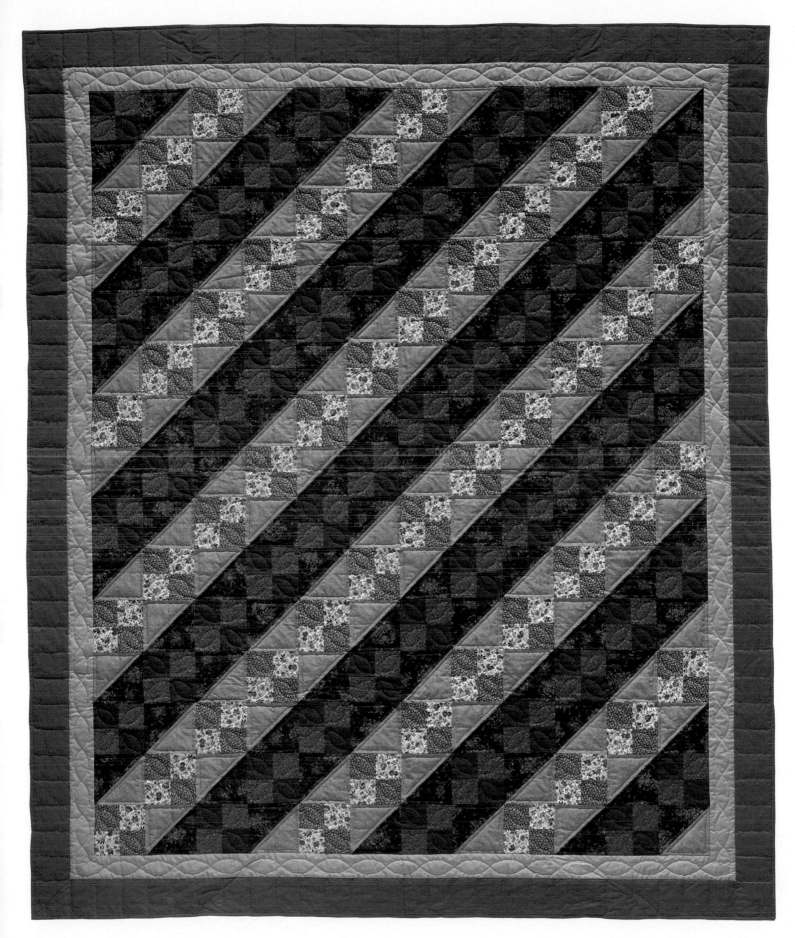

Four-Patch Quilting Pattern

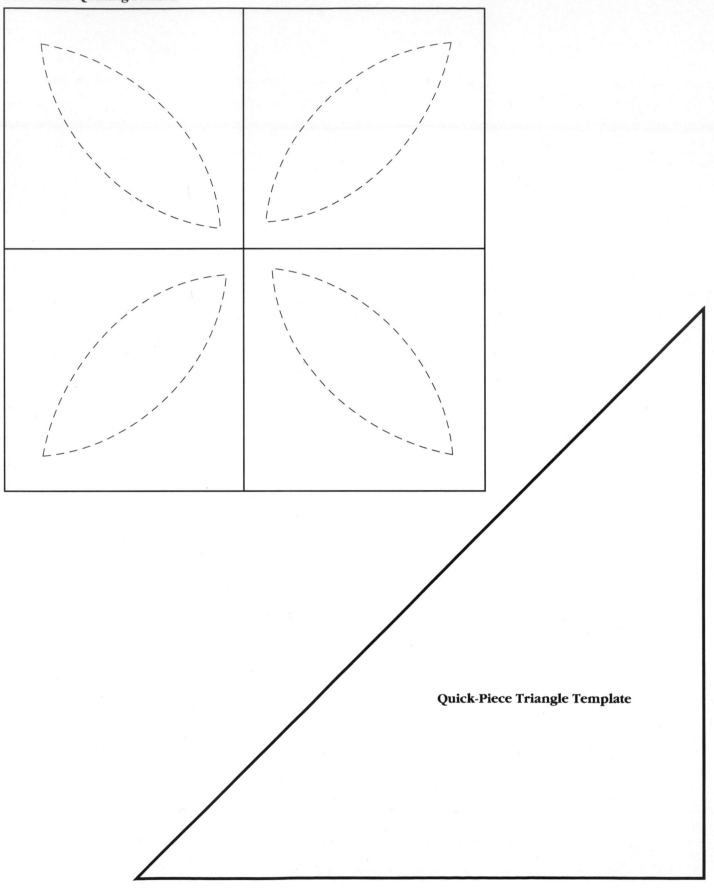

Quick-Piece Triangle Template

Inner Border Quilting Pattern

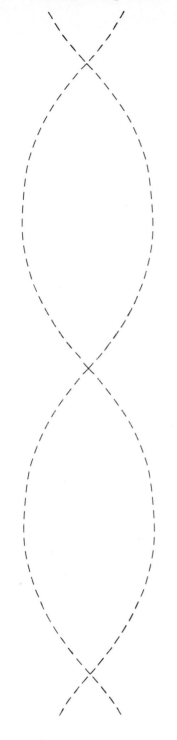

Enlarging Patterns

Because the full-size patterns do not fit the pages in this book, five of the projects in the following chapters require that you enlarge the patterns. But don't panic! There are several ways of doing this that require just a little extra time to accomplish.

All large cities and many small towns have photocopy shops where you can have photocopies made for a small fee. These same shops will enlarge or reduce a pattern for you. Just take the book to the shop and show the clerk the pattern that you want enlarged. Information printed with the pattern will tell what percentage to enlarge the design.

If no copy shop is available, or if you prefer to do your own enlarging, the process is really quite simple. First, draw a grid. Information with each gridded design will tell what size the squares of the grid should be. For instance, the Folk Horse Favorite pattern on page 69 is shown on a grid of 1″ squares. (See Figure 1 of diagram.) The instructions with the pattern tell you that 1 square equals 2″. That means you should draw a grid of 2″ squares. The easiest way to do this is to use graph paper or gridded freezer paper, which is already gridded with ⅛″ or ¼″ squares. (If you use gridded freezer paper, you can enlarge your pattern and draw your template at the same time. Freezer-paper templates can be pressed onto fabric with a warm iron, used as cutting guides, and then peeled off and used again. See "Freezer-Paper Appliqué" on page 58 for more information on using freezer-paper patterns.)

Now copy the design freehand, one square at a time, from the gridded pattern onto your drawn grid. (See Figure 2.) Since you are drawing such small segments, it is not necessary that you be an expert at sketching in order to enlarge patterns in this way.

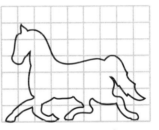

Figure 1: Original Pattern
1″ Squares

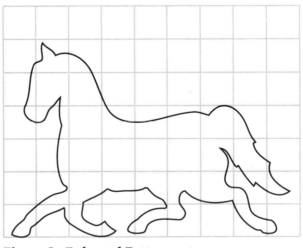

Figure 2: Enlarged Pattern
2″ Squares

• • •

By early summer, the wisteria has climbed the trellises to paint its green and purple signature around Marie's white clapboard house. Marie is Mama's best friend, and today half a dozen ladies have come together at her house for a quilting party.

My sister and I are the only children at this grown-up gathering where ladies, while they quilt, are apt to talk about matters unsuited to our young ears. So says Mama. Thus we have been assigned to the front porch swing where we are quite content to enjoy Marie's iced tea and tea cakes and pretend we are princesses at a garden party.

When we get bored with that, we're allowed to transfer our pretendings to the side yard where Marie's husband has hung a huge canvas hammock between two oaks. The hammock becomes an airplane in which we travel to wonderfully far places. Now it is a covered wagon carrying us westward, through every hardship we've ever witnessed at a Saturday afternoon picture show. Now it is a spaceship, blasting us millions of miles past Pluto.

By late afternoon we've exhausted our supply of imaginings, and we wander inside to where the ladies are still at work, making row upon row of stitches while discussing subjects that my sister and I hope to be old enough someday to discuss. Our presence reminds them of the time, and they prepare to leave the party. They'll return at the same time next week, though, to take up where they left off. For so they spend their summer leisure, bonding friendships with tiny stitches.

STENCILED TREASURES

Save time! Use this centuries-old craft to embellish quilt tops and quickly give them the delicate look of embroidery or appliqué.

Stenciling Quilts

Although not nearly as prevalent as piecing and appliqué, stenciling has been used to embellish quilt tops since the early 19th century. For those who don't have the time to create a quilt lavishly decorated with appliqué or embroidery, stenciling can provide similar effects in far less time. And it's worth trying, even if time is no object. Stenciled quilts have their own unique look, and it's quite appealing.

Stenciling is not a difficult craft. But if you aren't an experienced stenciler, practice a bit on scrap fabric to become familiar with the technique before beginning your quilt.

Materials

If you are planning to make a stenciled quilt, you'll need first to assemble the following basic tools and materials:

Mylar or other clear plastic sheets	Transparent tape
Masking tape	Acrylic craft paints
No. 2 lead pencil	Shallow dish
Craft knife	Blunt-bristle stencil brushes
Plate glass or other hard cutting surface	Paper towels

Making Stencils

Cut a piece of mylar large enough to accommodate your stencil design, allowing at least a 1″ margin all around the design. This is your *plate*. (The plate is always a square or a rectangle, regardless of the shape of the stencil design.)

Lay the plate over the stencil design, tape it in place, and trace the design with a sharp pencil. For designs with more than one color, cut a separate stencil for each color. (So that you can align each section, trace the entire design on each plate, but cut out only the areas to be stenciled with one color.) Assign each color a number and number each stencil accordingly.

To cut out the design, work on a hard surface, such as a piece of plate glass with the edges taped. (I do not advise the use of a rotary-cutting mat for cutting stencils, as the craft knife could damage the mat.) Use a sharp craft knife, holding the knife firmly and pulling it toward you. Cut out the smaller design elements first, keeping all edges as smooth as possible. Patch any miscuts with transparent tape.

Stenciling Your Design

Pour a small amount of paint into a shallow dish. Dip the end of your brush into the paint. Dab the bristles on several layers of clean paper towels to blot the excess paint. Work with as dry a brush as possible to ensure a sharp outline.

Tape your stencil securely in place. Working from the outside of each cut area in, apply the paint with a light tapping motion, straight up and down. The tips of the brush bristles should meet the surface head-on. (This technique is known as "pouncing.") When you've finished, carefully lift the stencil and wipe it clean with a wet paper towel.

Stencil one color at a time. Let the paint dry between colors. Use the uncut outline of the first color areas to register (or align) the stencil for the second color. Clean your stencils and brushes with soap and warm water.

After the stenciled design is dry, set the paints by pressing the back of the fabric with a medium-hot dry iron.

Sponging

Using a sponge instead of a brush to paint your stencil design produces a dappled effect. Any type of sponge will do, including manufactured sponges, but the best kind is the natural cosmetic sponge, available at drugstores, department stores, and many craft stores.

Thin the paint slightly with water in a shallow dish. Dip the sponge in the paint; then squeeze it to distribute the paint evenly through the sponge and to remove the excess. Stencil your design, touching the sponge on the fabric in a light, almost timid, dabbing motion.

Finishing Touches

Various methods can be used to enhance your stenciled design. Try a few well-placed embroidered details such as the French knot eyes of the butterflies in *Yellow Butterflies,* page 39, or add laces, ribbons, or other trims (see *Winter Skaters,* page 46).

Outline-quilt around selected areas of the stenciled design, either with matching or contrasting thread.

Yellow Butterflies

Bright butterflies, stenciled on white panels, embellish this tied quilt that can be made in a day.

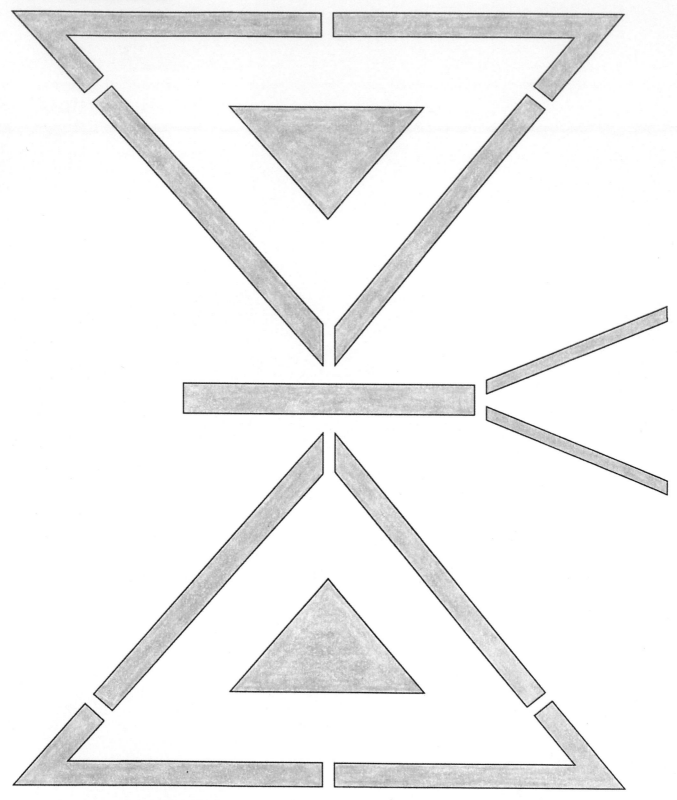

Finished Size
Quilt: 70" x 81"

Fabrics and Materials
White	2⅜ yards
Yellow print	2⅜ yards
Green solid for backing	5⅛ yards

8½" x 11" sheet of mylar
Craft knife
Yellow stencil paint
Medium stencil brush
Black embroidery floss

Instructions
1. See Making Stencils, page 38, to prepare stencil from pattern on page 40. Set stencil aside.

2. Cut 3 (10½" x 81½") strips from white fabric and 4 (10½" x 81½") strips from yellow print. Set yellow print strips aside.

3. Referring to Quilt Top Assembly diagram, stencil butterflies, evenly spaced, down length of each white strip. (See Stenciling Your Design, page 38.)

4. Follow Quilt Top Assembly diagram to join stenciled strips to yellow print strips.

5. Prepare backing to extend 2¼" beyond all sides of quilt top. Using 3 strands of floss, make French knots for butterfly eyes through all layers; embroider simple butterfly design (see photograph) at regular intervals through all layers across quilt.

Fold backing to front of quilt to form 1" self binding, turn under raw edge ¼", and slipstitch.

Quilt Top Assembly

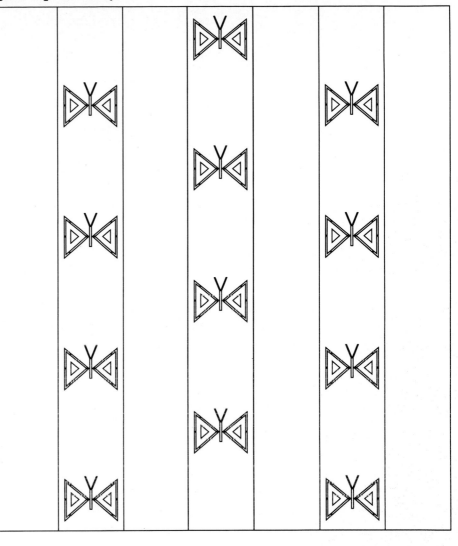

Flower Basket Star

Baskets of flowers stenciled in the centers of Evening Star blocks give the intricate look of appliqué or embroidery without the intricate work. The blocks can be pieced in short order by using your rotary-cutting tools, your sewing machine, and the quick-piece triangle method. And instead of being quilted, layers are tied together at intervals with lengths of crochet cotton.

Finished Sizes
Quilt: 92½″ x 110½″
Blocks: 20 (18″) Star Blocks

Fabrics and Materials

White	3 yards
Rose print	5 yards
Khaki print	5 yards
Backing	10¼ yards

3 (9½″-square) and 2 (3″ x 5″) sheets of mylar
Craft knife
Stencil paint: rose, green, brown
Small stencil brush
Rose crochet cotton

Instructions

1. See Making Stencils, page 38, to prepare stencils, using the 3 (9½″-square) sheets of mylar for the Flower Basket Stencil on page 44 and the 2 (3″ x 5″) sheets for the Flower Border Stencil on page 45. Set stencils aside.

2. Cut 20 (9½″) squares of white fabric. Set aside.

3. To make quick-piece triangles, cut 2 (37⅝″) squares each from rose print and khaki print and 1 (21½″ x

Flower Basket Star Block

37⅝″) rectangle each from rose print and khaki print.

Refer to Quick-Piece Triangle Method diagram on page 32 to mark and cut triangles as follows: With right sides facing and raw edges aligned, place 1 rose print square on top of 1 khaki print square. Use Quick-Piece Triangle Template on page 45 to trace 98 triangles onto fabric in manner shown in Figure 1. Machine-stitch ¼″ on either side of drawn diagonal lines as shown in Figure 2. Cut apart along drawn horizontal and vertical lines to form 2-layer squares as shown in Figure 3. Cut squares apart on drawn diagonal lines between lines of stitching to form 2-layer triangles as shown in Figures 4 and 5. Unfold triangles to form double-triangle squares (see Figure 6). Repeat Step 3 with remaining rose print and khaki print squares.

With right sides facing and raw edges aligned, place rose print rectangle on top of khaki print rectangle. Use quick-piece triangle method to trace and cut 44 more triangles, for a total of 240 double-triangle squares.

4. See Stenciling Your Design, page 38, to stencil Flower Basket on each of the 20 (9½″) white squares.

5. Follow block diagram to make 20 Flower Basket Star blocks, using double-triangle squares and stenciled Flower Basket squares.

6. Assemble blocks in 5 horizontal rows of 4 blocks each. Join rows.

7. Cut 2 (3½″-wide) border strips from khaki print and join to sides of quilt. Cut 2 (3½″-wide) border strips from khaki print and join to top and bottom of quilt.

Flower baskets have been popular quilt designs for more than 100 years. Stenciling is much faster than either embroidery or appliqué—but the results are just as striking, as the quilt at the right attests.

Flower Basket Stencil

8. From white fabric, cut 2 (3″-wide) border strips to match length of quilt. Cut 2 more (3″-wide) border strips to match length of quilt plus 5½″. Stencil Flower Border design, evenly spaced, down length of each strip. Join 2 long strips to sides of quilt. Join 2 short strips to top and bottom of quilt.

9. Cut 4 (5¼″-wide) border strips from rose print and join to sides of quilt, mitering corners.

10. Prepare backing to extend 2¼″ beyond all sides of quilt top. Using 4 strands of crochet cotton, tie quilt at centers of khaki and rose print squares and at corners of stenciled squares (see photograph).

Fold backing to front of quilt to form 1″ self binding, turn under raw edge ¼″, and slipstitch.

**Quick-Piece
Triangle
Template**

Flower Border Stencil

Quilt Top Assembly

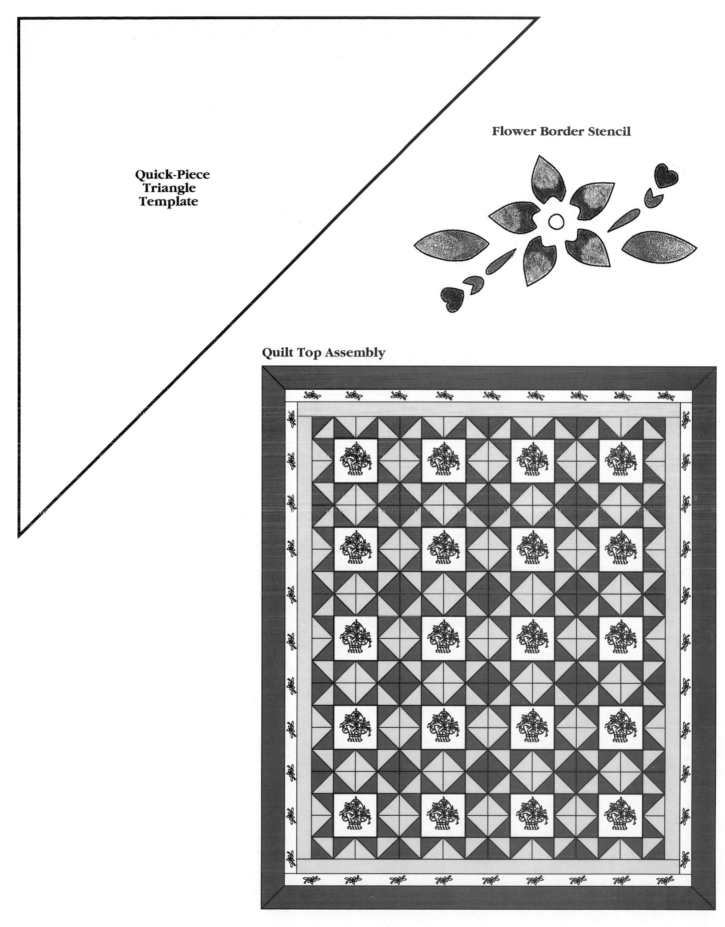

Winter Skaters

Betsy Freeman, the creator of these charming stenciled pieces, discovered the designs many years ago at a church bazaar. They were stenciled on a tablecloth that was being used to display jams and jellies. The tablecloth's owner, Sue Brown, gave Betsy permission to use the designs. The original tablecloth was created by Sue's mother, Fanny Burghalter, in the 1930s.

You will note that on some pieces, a figure will appear in reverse of its position on another piece. You can reverse any figure simply by turning the stencil over and applying paint from the back side.

Materials for All Pieces
Clear mylar for stencils
Craft knife
Stencil paints in colors of your choice*
Stencil brushes
Black fine-line permanent marker**

*Refer to photographs and patterns for suggested colors.
**If using a new marker, remove top and let air-dry for 20 minutes before using on fabric. Trace design with quick strokes because marker may bleed if held in place too long.

SKATERS ON THE LAKE

Finished Size
18″ x 47″

Fabrics and Materials
Muslin	⅝ yard
Floral print	1½ yards
Backing	1¾ yards

3⅝ yards (⅞″-wide) flat ecru lace

Instructions
1. Following photograph above, choose stencil designs from those on pages 48–52 and prepare stencils.

(See Making Stencils, page 38.)

2. Cut a 12½″ x 41½″ muslin rectangle. Stencil skaters on muslin. (See Stenciling Your Design, page 38.) Using marker, trace black detail lines on designs and draw facial features. Also fill in solid black areas on skates and fur trim.

3. Cut 2 (3½″-wide) border strips from floral print and join to top and bottom of stenciled panel. Cut 2 (3½″-wide) border strips and join to sides of stenciled panel.

4. Handstitch lace border around inner edge of floral print border, mitering corners (see photograph).

5. To make hanging loops, cut 5 (3½″ x 12½″) strips from floral print. With right sides facing, join the 2 long edges of 1 strip to form a tube. Turn. Press flat, with seam centered on back of strip. Fold strip in half. Repeat to make 4 more loops. With raw edges aligned and loops pointing toward center of quilt, baste loops to top edge on right side of quilt top.

6. Layer top, right side up; backing, right side down; and batting. (Use fleece, cotton flannel, or other low-loft batting for best results.) With batting against feed dogs if using non-woven batting, join edges, leaving a 6″ opening. Turn through opening. Slipstitch opening closed.

7. Outline-quilt skaters, including detail lines drawn with black marker. Quilt in-the-ditch along seam that joins stenciled panel to borders. Quilt hills in background as desired, referring to photograph for inspiration.

8. Tie bow with remaining lace and tack to side of quilt (see photograph).

50

*T*he wall
hanging on the
facing page will
bring a bit of old-
fashioned charm
to your home for
the holidays.
The designs are
from the 1930s.

A TRIO OF SKATERS

Finished Size
24½″ x 24½″

Fabrics and Materials
Muslin ½ yard
1 preprinted fabric square*
(approximately 25″)
Backing ¾ yard
Black embroidery floss
2⅝ yards (1″-wide) flat ecru lace
2¾ yards (⅛″-wide) ribbon
Red quilting thread
*Check decorator section of fabric store.

Instructions
1. Following photograph at right, choose stencil designs from those on pages 48–52 and prepare stencils. (See Making Stencils, page 38.)
2. Cut a 14″ square and 2 (5″ x 9″) rectangles of muslin. Stencil skater trio on square. Stencil 1 corner skater on each rectangle. (See Stenciling Your Design, page 38.) Use marker to trace black detail lines on designs and to draw facial features. Also fill in solid black areas on skates and fur trim.
3. Cut a 13½″ window in center of preprinted square. Center stenciled square behind window and baste in place. Turn under ¼″ along window's raw edge and slipstitch to stenciled square.
4. Cut corner skaters from muslin, leaving ¼″ seam allowance. Turn under raw edges and appliqué to bottom left and upper right corners (see photograph). Using 2 strands of floss, outline corner skaters with stem-stitch. Handstitch lace in place on quilt about ¼″ outside edge of sten-ciled square, tying bows at 3 corners as shown in photograph.
5. Cut a 25″ square of backing. Fol-low Step 6 of Skaters on the Lake, page 47.
6. With red quilting thread, outline-quilt skaters as shown in pho-tograph. Quilt in-the-ditch along seam where stenciled square joins pre-printed square. Quilt along lines of preprinted square as desired.
7. Tie ribbon bows and tack to cor-ners as shown.

SOLO SKATER

Finished Size
19″ x 23″

Fabrics and Materials

White	¼ yard
Blue pindot	⅜ yard
Muslin	¼ yard
Floral stripe	¾ yard
Backing	¾ yard

1 yard (⅛″-wide) navy ribbon
1¾ yards (½″-wide) flat ecru lace
Black embroidery floss

Instructions

1. Following photograph at right, choose stencil design from those on pages 48–52 and prepare stencils. (See Making Stencils, page 38.)

2. Cut a 7½″ x 12½″ rectangle from white and a 9½″ x 12½″ rectangle from blue pindot. With right sides facing and 1 long raw edge of white fabric aligned with 1 long raw edge of blue fabric, lay white rectangle on top of blue rectangle. Join along aligned edge, forming gently curving seam as shown in photograph. Trim seam to ¼″. Clip curves and press seam toward blue. Topstitch ¼″ from seam on blue. Set unit aside.

3. Cut a 5″ x 10″ rectangle from muslin. Stencil skater on muslin. (See Stenciling Your Design, page 38.) Use marker to trace black detail lines and draw facial features. Also fill in solid black areas on fur trim. Cut out skater, leaving ¼″ seam allowance. Turn under seam allowance and appliqué skater to pieced unit as shown in photograph. Using 2 strands of floss, outline skater with stemstitch.

4. Cut 4 (4″-wide) border strips from floral stripe fabric and join to sides of quilt, mitering corners.

5. Handstitch lace along seam line where border joins appliquéd panel (see photograph).

6. Follow Step 6 of Skaters on the Lake, page 47.

7. Outline-quilt skater. Quilt along lines of floral stripe as desired.

8. Tie ribbon in bow and tack to upper left corner, with ends draping, as shown in photograph.

SKATERS PLACE MAT

Finished Size
12½" x 17½"

Fabrics
Muslin .... ⅜ yard
Floral print .... ⅛ yard
Solid .... Scraps
Backing .... ½ yard

Instructions

1. Following photograph below, choose stencil designs from those on pages 48–52 and prepare stencils. (See Making Stencils, page 38.)

2. Cut 10" x 15" rectangle from muslin. Stencil skaters on muslin. (See Stenciling Your Design, page 38.) Use marker to trace black detail lines on designs and draw facial features. Also fill in solid black areas on skates.

3. Cut 2 (2" x 10") and 2 (2" x 15") strips from floral print. Cut 4 (2") squares from solid scraps. Join 1 square to each end of each of the 2 (2" x 15") strips. Join 2" x 10" strips to sides of stenciled panel. Join strips with squares to top and bottom of panel.

4. Layer batting; top, right side up; and backing, right side down. With batting against feed dogs, join around edges, leaving a 6" opening. Turn through opening. Slipstitch opening closed.

5. Outline-quilt skaters, including detail lines drawn with black marker, as shown in photograph. Quilt in-the-ditch along border seam line.

*H*appy children, bundled against the cold, skate across this place mat, which was stenciled and stitched in soft shades of blue, brown, and rose.

CHAPTER THREE

Cold, wet January has intruded upon our lives, my sister's and mine. It has brought with it ice to keep us inside, cold floors to keep us in shoes, and, finally, measles to keep us in bed.

Mama hangs heavy blankets across the bedroom window, shutting out every hint of daylight that she says could harm our eyes, which are in a weakened state from the measles. She makes us drink gallons of a brown fiery drink called Buffalo Rock. It's supposed to make us break out. She and Daddy sit with us all night while we whine and thrash—until our fevers break at dawn and they know all will be well with their two youngest.

In the days ahead as we mend, we resent our imprisonment in bed—the same bed for us both because my little sister cries if they try to separate us. Finally we're allowed to sit up and occupy our minds with make-believe. We ask for books, but Mama says we mustn't strain our eyes. She does, however, bring us our two shoeboxes, each one filled with pieces from dozens of paperdoll books, cut for us by our older sister.

Our bed is covered by a thick comforting quilt whose pattern I cannot remember now. But I do recall its fabrics. Atop the quilt, among the prints of birds, beasts, and flowers, we build a wonderland with our paperdolls and live out lives for them that take us out of the world of our illness and keep us content until first, good health and later, sweet spring come to relieve us of our housebound confinement and set us free again.

APPLIQUÉD PLEASURES

If you like to appliqué, you'll love the techniques in this chapter. They make appliqué quicker, easier, and more precise.

Quick-Appliqué Techniques

Here are some methods you can use to fit the intricate art of appliqué, often an extremely time-consuming handicraft, into a busy schedule. All the quilts in this chapter can be appliquéd using one of the following methods. As you can see, quality does not have to be sacrificed for the sake of time.

Machine Appliqué

Paper-backed fusible web is a great boon to the stitcher who wants to make quick work of appliqué. It allows you to fuse your appliqué design to your background fabric so that it will lie flat and not shift while you machine-stitch around it. Because edges are not turned under in machine appliqué, no seam allowances are added. Paper-backed fusible web is widely available at quilt, fabric, and craft shops.

Trace the patterns for the appliqué shapes onto tracing paper. (If a design is not symmetrical, you must turn the pattern over and trace a mirror image to use as your pattern. This will prevent your pattern from being reversed when applied to the wrong side of the fabric and cut out.)

Following manufacturer's instructions, fuse the web to the wrong side of the appliqué fabric. Then trace your appliqué shapes onto the paper side of the fusible web. Cut out the shapes on the outlines. Peel away the paper backing. Place the shapes, web side down, on the right side of your background fabric and fuse in place.

Place a piece of *lightweight paper* or *tear-away stabilizer* beneath the background fabric behind the appliqué shape. Using matching or contrasting sewing thread, as you prefer, finish the edges of your appliqué shapes with machine-satin stitch, a close-spaced zigzag. (Always stitch a sample first to be sure that your stitch length and width are satisfactory.) Tear the stabilizer from behind the figure.

Freezer-Paper Appliqué

Supermarket *freezer paper* can make hand appliqué much easier by giving you nice sharp corners and smooth edges to work with. (Gridded freezer paper, available at some quilt shops, gives you a handy grid for enlarging patterns or placing grain lines.) For smaller pieces, such as *Tranquility Rose,* page 64, and *Folk Horse Favorite,* page 66, you may want to spend the little extra time involved in handwork to achieve the desired effect.

Trace the patterns for the appliqué shapes onto tracing paper. (If a design is not symmetrical, you must turn the pattern over and trace a mirror image to use as your pattern. This will prevent your pattern from being reversed when applied to the wrong side of the fabric and cut out.)

Trace your appliqué shapes, without seam allowances, on the dull side of the freezer paper. Cut out the shapes on the outlines. Pin the shapes, shiny side down, to the wrong side of your fabric, spacing them at least ½" apart. Press in place with a hot, dry iron. Cut out the shapes, adding ¼" seam allowances. Clip curves almost to the edge of the paper.

Turn the seam allowances on the appliqué shapes to the dull side of the freezer paper and press or baste in place. Pin the shapes, paper side down, in place on the right side of the background fabric. Using a slipstitch, appliqué the shapes to the background fabric.

To remove the freezer paper, cut away the background fabric from behind the appliqué shapes, leaving ¼" seam allowances. Peel away the freezer paper. Cutting away the background fabric not only lets you remove the paper, but it also leaves less bulk through which to quilt.

Once the shapes are stitched in place, you can add an accent line of stemstitching or blanket stitching in a matching or contrasting thread, if desired.

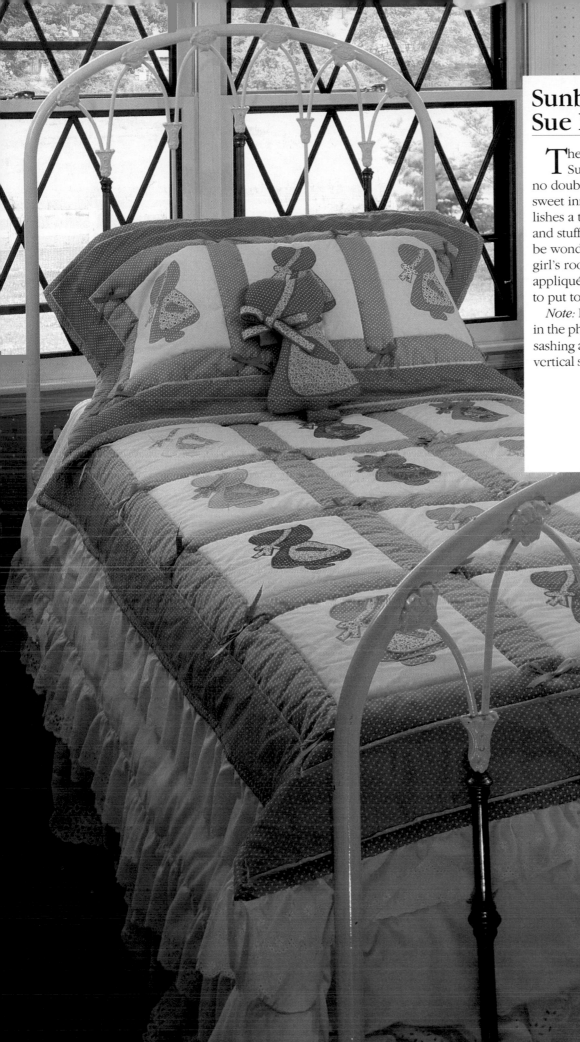

Sunbonnet Sue Lives!

The perennial popularity of the Sunbonnet Sue design is due, no doubt, to its simple lines and sweet innocence. Here Sue embellishes a twin-size quilt, pillow sham, and stuffed doll pillow that would be wonderful accents to any little girl's room. Fusible web and machine appliqué make these projects a snap to put together.

Note: If using directional prints as in the photograph, cut horizontal sashing and borders crosswise and vertical sashing and borders lengthwise.

Materials for All Pieces
Paper-backed fusible web
Tear-away stabilizer or white paper
Matching thread

RUFFLED QUILT

Finished Sizes
Quilt: 52" x 73"
Blocks: 10" x 12"

Fabrics and Materials
White	1⅛ yards
Green miniprint	1¾ yards
Pink miniprint	2⅛ yards
Yellow miniprint	½ yard
Assorted dk. miniprints	⅝ yard
Assorted lt. floral prints	¼ yard
Backing	4½ yards

6½ yards (⅜"-wide) satin ribbon in assorted colors
7½ yards (4½"-wide) pregathered white eyelet lace

Instructions
1. Referring to Machine Appliqué, page 58, use templates on page 61 to trace each piece (Sue, Hatband, Arm, and Apron) 12 times on paper side of fusible web. Cut web pieces apart. Iron web pieces to wrong sides of fabric—Sues and arms to dk. miniprints, hatbands and aprons to lt. floral prints. Cut out pieces on the outlines.

2. Cut 12 (10½" x 12½") rectangles from white fabric.

3. Center 1 Sue on 1 white rectangle and fuse in place. Fuse hatband and apron to Sue. Fuse arm to apron. Repeat for 11 remaining blocks.

4. Place stabilizer behind block. (Refer to Machine Appliqué, page 58.) Satin-stitch around each piece. (See photograph above.) Remove stabilizer. Repeat for remaining blocks.

5. Cut 9 (3½" x 10½") sashing strips from green miniprint and join blocks with sashing strips to form 3 (4-block) vertical rows. (See Quilt Top Assembly diagram on page 61.)
Cut 4 (3½" x 57½") sashing strips from green miniprint and join vertical

rows as shown in diagram. Cut 2 (3½" x 42½") strips from green miniprint and join to top and bottom of quilt.

6. Cut 9 (1½"-wide) strips across width of yellow miniprint. Piece strips to form 2 (1½" x 44"), 2 (1½" x 70"), 2 (1½" x 55"), and 2 (1½" x 74") strips. With wrong sides facing, press strips in half lengthwise to make piping.

With long raw edges aligned, join the 70" piping to sides of quilt. Join 44" piping to top and bottom of quilt. Trim ends of piping even with green sashing. Press piping toward center of quilt. Set remaining 4 piping strips aside.

7. From pink miniprint, cut 4 (4½"-wide) inner border strips and join to quilt as shown in Quilt Top Assembly diagram.

8. With long raw edges aligned, join (1½" x 74") piping to sides of quilt. Join (1½" x 55") piping to top

and bottom of quilt. Trim ends of piping even with inner border. Press piping toward center of quilt.

9. Cut 4 (1½"-wide) outer border strips from green miniprint and join to quilt as shown in Quilt Top Assembly diagram.

10. With right sides facing, edges aligned, and ruffle pointing toward center of quilt, join ruffled eyelet to quilt.

11. Layer batting; top, right side up; and backing, right side down. With batting against feed dogs, join layers along all sides, leaving an opening in top large enough to turn quilt. Turn quilt. Slipstitch opening closed.

12. Machine-quilt in-the-ditch around all blocks and sashing.

13. Cut ribbon into 20 (12") pieces. Tie each piece in a bow and tack bows to quilt as shown in photograph.

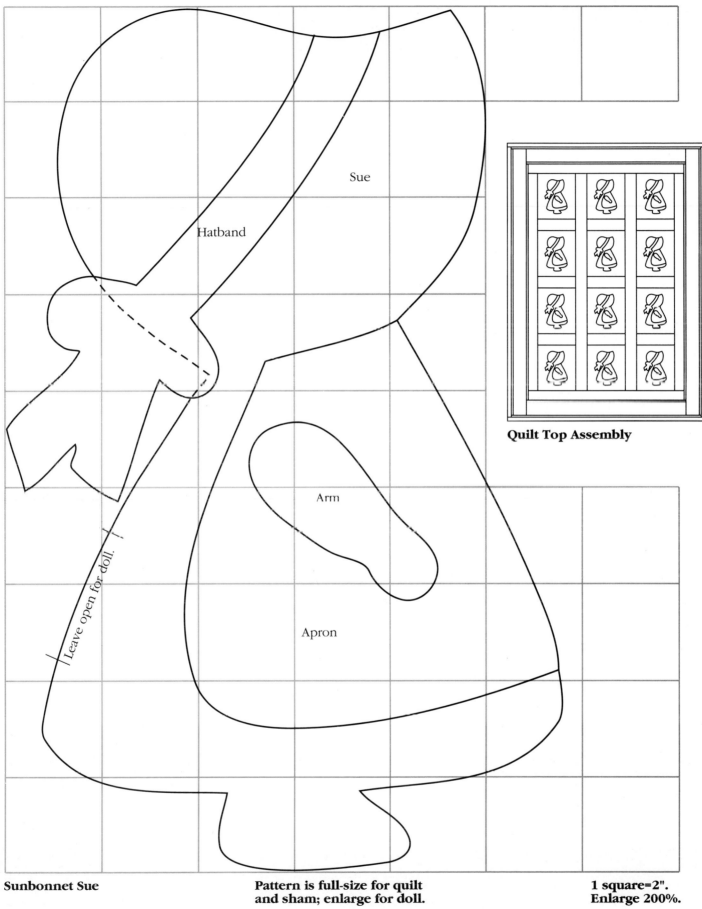

Quilt Top Assembly

Leave open for doll.

Sue

Hatband

Arm

Apron

Sunbonnet Sue

Pattern is full-size for quilt and sham; enlarge for doll.

**1 square=2".
Enlarge 200%.**

PILLOW SHAM OR WALL HANGING

Finished Sizes
Sham: 28" x 52"
Blocks: 10" x 12"

Fabrics and Materials

White	½ yard
Green miniprint	1½ yards
Yellow miniprint	¼ yard
Pink miniprint	1¼ yards
3 dk. miniprints: 7" x 10" scrap each	
3 lt. floral prints: 7" x 8" scrap each	
Backing	1⅝ yards

2¾ yards (⅜"-wide) pink satin ribbon

Instructions

1. Follow instructions for Ruffled Quilt, Step 1, on page 60, cutting 3 of each piece instead of 12.

2. Cut 3 (10½" x 12½") rectangles from white fabric.

3. Follow instructions for Ruffled Quilt, Steps 3 and 4.

4. Cut 4 (3½" x 12½") sashing strips from green miniprint and join to blocks to form horizontal row. (See photograph below.)

5. Cut 2 (3½" x 42½") sashing strips from green miniprint and join to top and bottom of row.

6. Cut 5 (1½"-wide) strips across width of yellow miniprint. Join pieces to form 1 long (1½"-wide) strip. With wrong sides facing, press strip in half lengthwise to make piping. With long raw edges aligned, join piping to sides of pillow sham, trimming ends of piping even with sashing as you join. Next, join piping to top and bottom of pillow sham, trimming ends of piping even with sashing. Press piping toward center of pillow sham.

7. Cut 4 (4½"-wide) inner border strips from pink miniprint and join to pillow sham as shown in photograph.

8. With raw edges aligned, join remaining piping to edges of pillow sham, trimming ends of piping even with border strips. Press piping toward center of pillow sham.

9. Cut 4 (1½"-wide) outer border strips from green miniprint and join to pillow sham.

10. Follow Ruffled Quilt, Steps 11 and 12.

11. Cut ribbon into 8 (12") pieces. Tie each piece in a bow and tack bows to pillow sham as shown in the photograph below.

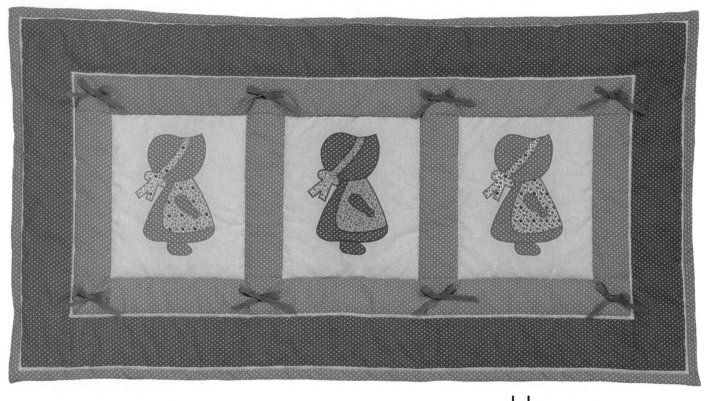

U*se the Sunbonnet Sue motif to make a wall hanging or a pillow sham to match the quilt (above). Or enlarge the pattern for a puffy doll pillow (facing page).*

STUFFED DOLL PILLOW

Finished Size
17″ high

Fabrics and Materials

Pink miniprint	⅔ yard
Lt. floral print	½ yard
Polyester stuffing	

Instructions

1. Enlarge Sunbonnet Sue pattern on page 61, omitting hatband. (See Enlarging Patterns, page 35.)

2. Use templates to trace 1 Sue and 1 reverse Sue on pink miniprint. Referring to Machine Appliqué, page 58, trace 1 arm and 1 apron on paper side of fusible web. Cut out Sues, adding ¼″ seam allowance. Cut apart web pieces and fuse to wrong side of fabrics—apron to lt. floral print, arm to pink miniprint. Cut out pieces on outlines. Fuse apron to Sue. Fuse arm to apron.

3. Place stabilizer behind Sue and satin-stitch around appliquéd Sue, ¼″ from edge along seam line. Satin-stitch outlines of fused-on pieces. (See photograph.) Remove stabilizer.

4. With right sides facing and raw edges aligned, join appliquéd Sue and reverse Sue, leaving opening as indicated on pattern. Turn. Stuff firmly. Slipstitch opening closed.

5. Cut 1 (3″-wide) strip across width of remaining lt. floral print. Cut 3″-wide strips of fusible web to match length of floral print strip. Fuse web to wrong side of floral print strip. With wrong sides facing and raw edges aligned, fold strip in half lengthwise. Fuse together. Satin-stitch edges of strip. (See photograph.) Tie strip in a bow around Sue's bonnet as shown in photograph.

Tranquility Rose

This small appliquéd piece is reminiscent of the many traditional rose designs, some of which date back to colonial times. Some of these, such as Democrat Rose and Radical Rose, became political statements. Others like Ohio Rose and Missouri Rose were symbols of regional pride.

Finished Size
17″ x 22″

Fabrics and Materials

Blue solid	⅜ yard
Yellow print	⅛ yard
Green print	⅛ yard
Green solid	⅛ yard
Peach solid	Scrap
Rose print	¼ yard
Lt. blue print	⅛ yard
Rose solid	¼ yard
Backing	½ yard
Freezer paper	

Instructions

1. Enlarge gridded pattern below. (See Enlarging Patterns, page 35.)

2. Cut 1 (11½″ x 16½″) rectangle from blue solid.

3. Refer to Freezer-Paper Appliqué, page 58, to cut appliqué pieces as indicated on pattern. Next, appliqué the

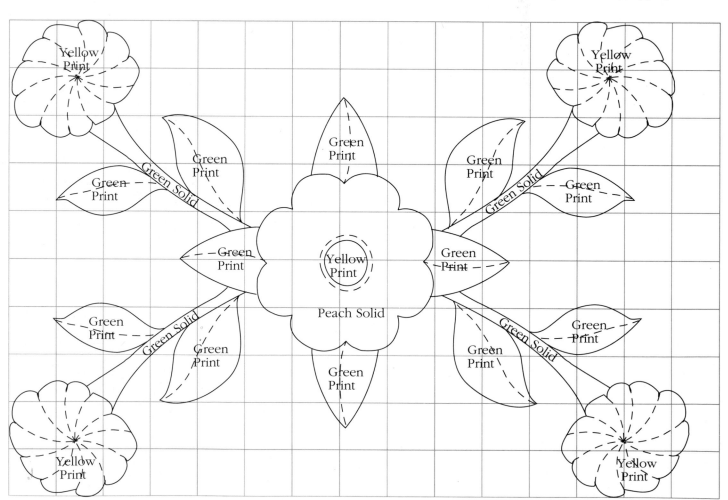

Tranquility Rose Appliqué
1 square= 1".
Enlarge 200%.

Tranquility Rose design to blue solid rectangle.

4. From rose print, cut 2 (3½″ x 16½″) border strips and 2 (3½″ x 11½″) border strips. From light blue print, cut 4 (3½″) squares. Join 3½″ x 16½″ strips to top and bottom of appliquéd block. Join 1 light blue square to each end of remaining rose print strips. Join strips to sides of block.

5. Outline-quilt around entire design. Add quilted details as shown on pattern. Bind with straight-grain binding made from rose solid.

The freezer-paper technique makes hand appliqué easier and helps ensure sharp corners and smooth edges. Muted shades of blue and rose add softness to this lyrical design.

Folk Horse Favorite

Freezer-paper appliqué makes quick work of the center panel of this charming country wall hanging. And although you might never guess it, the outer border is strip-pieced. Even the Turkey Track corner blocks are quick-stitched, using a combination of piecing and appliqué.

Finished Size
30" x 36"

Fabrics and Materials

Center panel	
background	⅝ yard
Horse appliqué	⅜ yard
Red pindot inner	
border	⅛ yard
Striped inner border	¾ yard
Corner Turkey Track blocks:	
Background	¼ yard
2 prints	⅛ yard each
Strip-pieced outer border:	
10 prints	⅛ yard each
Backing	1 yard
Black for binding	¼ yard
Freezer paper	

Instructions

1. Enlarge gridded pattern on page 69. (See Enlarging Patterns, page 35.)

2. Cut 1 (16½" x 22½") rectangle from center panel background fabric.

3. Refer to Freezer-Paper Appliqué, page 58, to cut out horse and appliqué to background.

4. Join inner borders as follows: Cut 3 (1¼"-wide) crosswise strips from red pindot and join, log cabin fashion, to the center panel. (See the Wall Hanging Assembly diagram below.) Cut 4 (2¼"-wide) border strips from striped fabric and join to the quilt, mitering the corners.

5. Make 4 Turkey Track blocks as follows: Cut 4 (5") squares from corner block background fabric. From the 2 prints, cut pieces A and B as indicated on templates on page 68.

Join 1 A and 1 B to make 1 Turkey Track. (See Wall Hanging Assembly diagram.) Center Turkey Track on 1 background square and appliqué. Repeat for 3 more blocks.

6. Make strip-pieced border as follows: Cut 21 (1½"-wide) crosswise strips from the 10 border prints, cutting 3 from 1 print and 2 from each of the remaining 9 prints. Join strips along long edges, alternating order of prints, to form striped unit. (See Strip-Pieced Border Construction diagram on page 68.) Press all seams in same direction.

Cut 5 (5"-wide) strip-pieced border pieces from striped unit as shown in diagram. (Reserve remainder of striped unit for another project.)

Join 1 strip-pieced border each to right and left sides of quilt. Since remaining strip-pieced border units are

Wall Hanging Assembly

Turkey Track — Block

A *prancing horse, reminiscent of an old-fashioned weather vane, is the subject of this wall quilt. The appliqué, corner block, and striped border all use quick-quilting techniques.*

not long enough for top and bottom of quilt, separate enough stripes (approximately 6 for each) from fifth strip-pieced unit and join to remaining borders to make them long enough to fit across top and bottom of quilt.

Join 1 Turkey Track block to each end of each of these remaining strip-pieced borders. Join borders to top and bottom of quilt.

7. Quilt 2 parallel rows around horse. Quilt just inside seam line of center panel. Quilt just inside seam line on each side of inner borders. Quilt ⅛″ from edge of quilt all around. Bind with ½″-wide straight-grain binding made from black fabric.

Strip-Pieced Border Construction

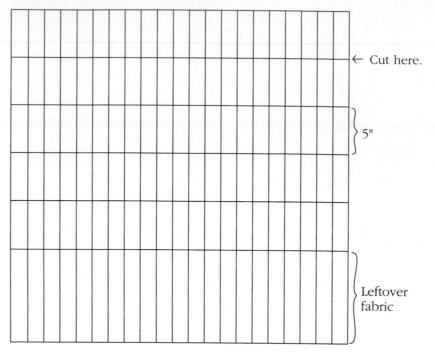

← Cut here.

} 5″

} Leftover fabric

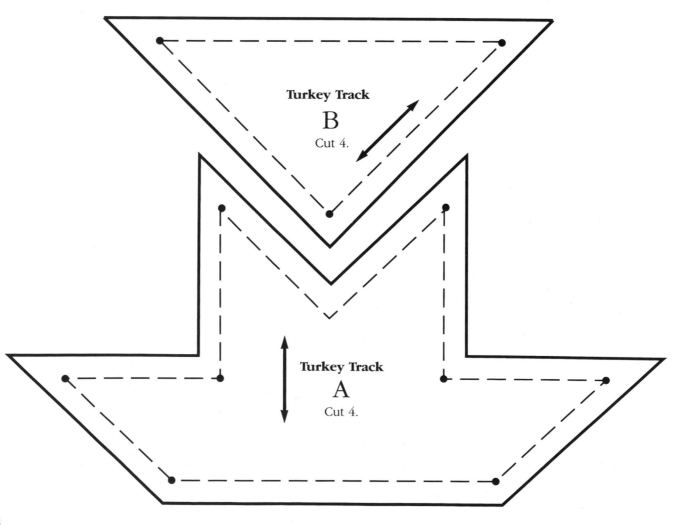

Turkey Track

B

Cut 4.

Turkey Track

A

Cut 4.

Folk Horse Appliqué
1 Square = 2".
Enlarge 200%.

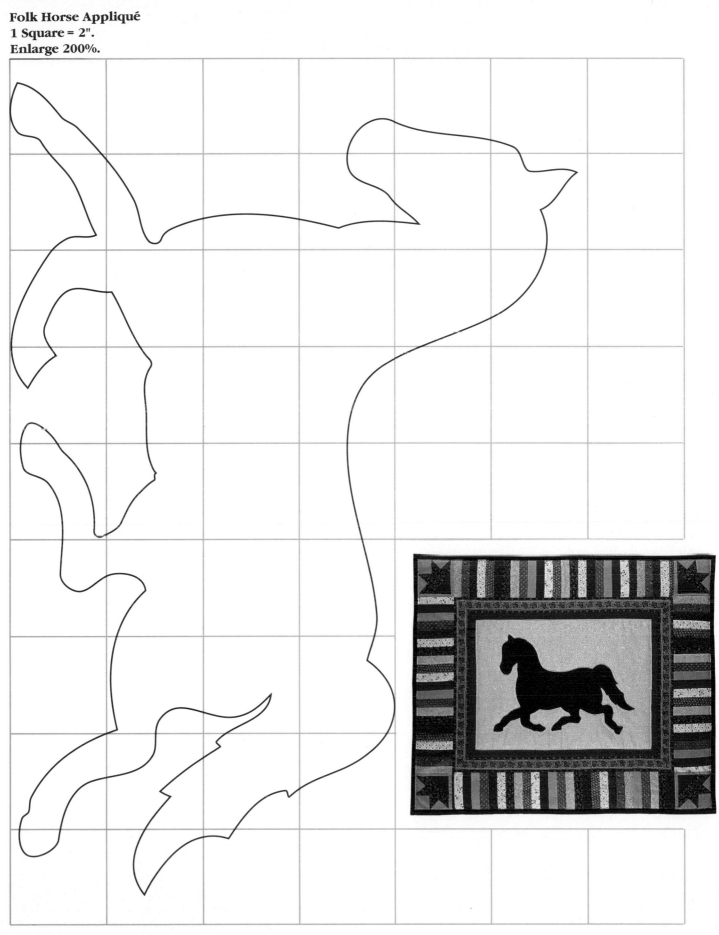

Heart's Desire

Using easy machine appliqué and machine quilting "by the block," you'll have this appliquéd quilt finished before you know it.

Finished Sizes
Quilt: 76" x 95"
Blocks: 20 (19") Heart Blocks

Fabrics and Materials
White   5½ yards
Assorted prints   4 yards
Backing   5½ yards
7¾ yards paper-backed fusible web
Tear-away stabilizer or white paper

Instructions
   1. Cut 20 (19½") squares from white. Set aside.
   2. Referring to Machine Appliqué, page 58, use Heart Appliqué pattern below to trace 80 hearts on paper side of fusible web. Cut web hearts apart. Iron web hearts to wrong sides of assorted prints. Cut out the fabric

Heart Appliqué

Puffy hearts, cut from assorted prints and machine-appliquéd to white blocks, form this country charmer. The quilting patterns on page 73 were designed especially for machine quilting.

Heart's Desire Block

Joining Prequilted Blocks

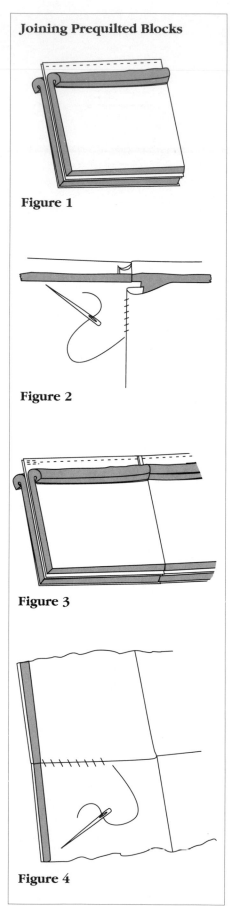

Figure 1

Figure 2

Figure 3

Figure 4

hearts on the drawn outlines.

3. Following Heart's Desire Block diagram for placement, fuse 4 hearts to each white square. Place stabilizer behind 1 block and satin-stitch around each heart. Remove stabilizer. Repeat for remaining blocks.

4. Cut backing fabric into 20 (19½″) squares. Cut batting into 20 (19½″) squares.

5. Layer 1 backing square, right side down; batting; and 1 Hearts Desire block, right side up. Following block diagram for placement, transfer quilting designs on page 73 to block. Machine-quilt. (See Machine Quilting, page 9.) Repeat for remaining 19 blocks.

6. Refer to Joining Prequilted Blocks diagram to join blocks as follows: With backing and batting rolled back and pinned, lay 2 blocks together with top sides facing. (See Figure 1.) Join with machine stitching. Remove pins. Continue joining blocks until you have formed a horizontal row of 4 blocks.

With backing side up, lay row on flat surface. Finger-press seams in the same direction. (From row to row, alternate direction of seams.) Trim batting so that 2 pieces abut. With 1 edge of backing lying flat, turn other edge under ¼″ and slipstitch lapped seam closed. (See Figure 2.) Repeat to make 4 more rows.

7. Join rows as follows: With backing and batting rolled back and pinned, lay 2 rows together with top sides facing and vertical seams matching. (See Figure 3.) Join with machine stitching, backstitching at each end. Join remaining rows in same manner.

With backing side up, lay quilt on flat surface. Finger-press each seam in the same direction. Trim batting so that 2 pieces abut. With 1 edge of backing lying flat, turn other edge under ¼″ and slipstitch lapped seam closed. (See Figure 4.) Repeat for remaining backing seams.

8. Cut scraps from assorted prints into 2½″-wide bias strips. Join strips to make 9½ yards of bias binding. With wrong sides facing, press binding in half lengthwise. Bind quilt.

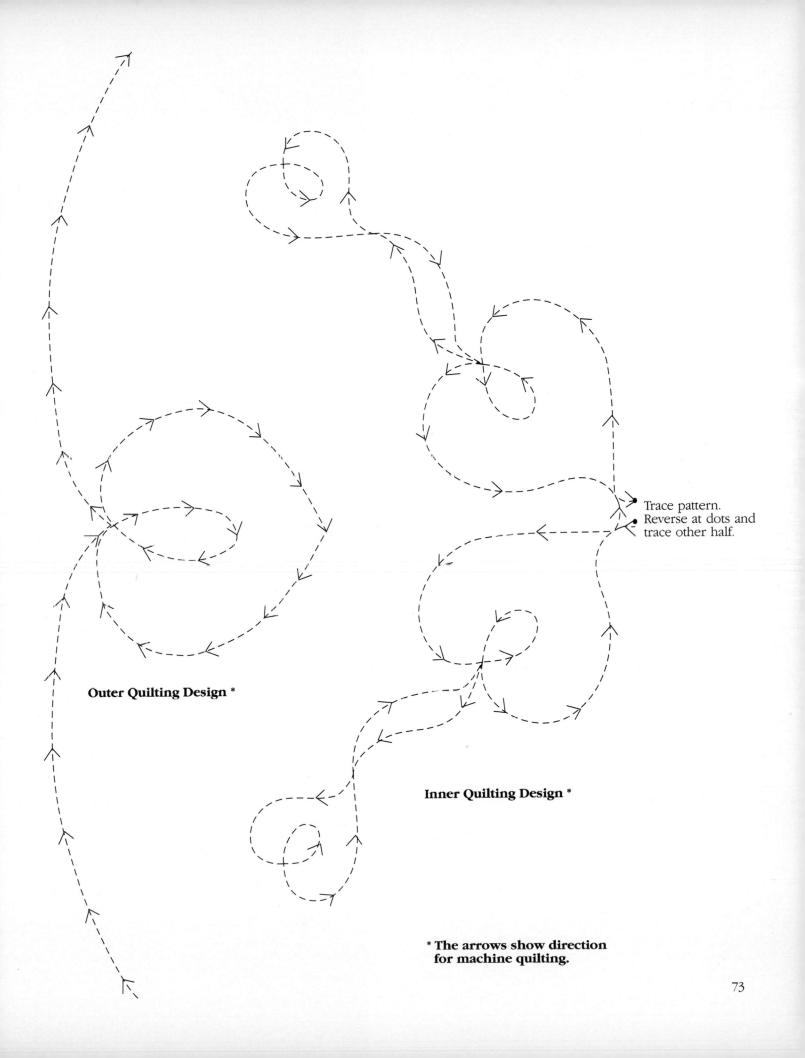

Trace pattern.
Reverse at dots and
trace other half.

Outer Quilting Design *

Inner Quilting Design *

* **The arrows show direction
for machine quilting.**

• • •

CHAPTER FOUR

J ust when I first donned a thimble and took up a needle to stitch, I do not now remember. I do recall hating the thimble and tossing it aside when Mama wasn't looking. She always found out, though, and insisted that I return the thimble to my finger and learn to sew the proper way.

When my own children were old enough to express an interest in needle and thread, I came to appreciate the trials that Mama suffered as she tried to guide my clumsy childish hands into something resembling fine stitches. After embroidering a pillowcase to the knee of her blue jeans and producing a solid clump of knots with her crochet, my daughter one day decided she was sufficiently experienced to graduate to the art of quilting. I chose a pattern for her, a simple Four Patch made up of two-inch squares. I drafted a template, and we set to work. She chose some favorite pieces from my scrap bag and patiently went about drawing and cutting out squares. Several attempts had to be discarded for lack of straight lines, but she persevered.

She cut and pieced and ripped out and repieced for several days, long after her childhood fervor had cooled. I believe she did not want to disappoint me by giving up on what she knew to be a passion of mine. But finally her will grew weak, and the games that her brother and his friends were engaged in outside became too big a draw. She deserted her quilt.

But inside a drawer of memories, underneath pieces of old lace, black-and-white photographs, and yellowing greeting cards, lie three little quilt blocks that are worth more to me than yards of Irish linen.

WHOLE-CLOTH HANDIWORK

Large, unpieced sections of fabric can help you make the most of your quilting time. Some fabrics are even preprinted with traditional quilt-block patterns.

Preprinted Patchwork

Those pretty preprinted quilt blocks that line fabric store racks are good for more than making pillows, tote bags, and apron bibs. They make wonderful quick quilts, too! The two quilts here show how preprinted blocks can be used to add handmade warmth to any room in your house without spending the time to make hand-pieced blocks.

Preprinted blocks come in dozens of designs. Some are reproductions or variations of traditional quilt block patterns, and some are original designs. They are available in a range of decorator colors. And for most, co-ordinating prints and solids are available that can be used for sashing, borders, or backing; or they can be used for making accent pieces such as pillows, tablecloths, or curtains.

Usually printed four to the yard, preprinted quilt blocks come with generous borders that allow several different block designs to be trimmed to a uniform size for use in sampler quilts such as this one. Here the quilter added two-inch navy sashing to frame the blocks. Strategically placed quilting lines make the blocks appear to be hand-pieced.

Twenty repetitions of the same block were set together with three-inch muslin sashing and borders to make this floral beauty. The block design is reminiscent of the 18th-century technique of broderie perse, *a method of cutting designs from chintz or other elaborately printed fabric and appliquéing them onto a plain background. The pillow shams and table cover are made from coordinating print fabric.*

The Night Before Christmas

Six Evening Star blocks, pieced in red and green miniprints, alternate with six preprinted blocks for a festive wall hanging that tells the story of "The Night Before Christmas." But any preprinted Christmas block will do. The following instructions are for 12½" blocks (unfinished size). If necessary, trim or piece your preprinted blocks to 12½".

Finished Sizes
Quilt: 40" x 52"
Blocks: 6 (12") Preprinted Blocks
       6 (12") Evening Star Blocks

Fabrics
6 preprinted Christmas blocks
Red print   ¾ yard
Green print   ½ yard
Muslin   ½ yard
Backing   1⅝ yards

Instructions

1. Cut out preprinted blocks and set aside.

2. Make 6 Evening Star blocks as follows: Cut 18 (3⅞") squares from red print. Cut squares in half diagonally to form 36 half-square triangles. (See Making Half-Square and Quarter-Square Triangles, page 5.) Cut 12 (3½") corner squares from red print.

From green print, cut 18 (3⅞") squares. Cut squares in half diagonally to form 36 half-square triangles. Cut 12 (3½") corner squares from green print.

From muslin, cut 36 (3⅞") squares. Cut squares in half diagonally to form 72 half-square triangles.

Follow block diagrams below to make 3 Block 1s and 3 Block 2s.

3. Follow the Quilt Top Assembly diagram below to set preprinted blocks and Evening Star blocks together in 4 horizontal rows of 3 blocks each. Join rows.

4. From red print, cut 4 (2½" x 17½") border strips and 4 (2½" x 23½") border strips. From green print, cut 8 (2½") squares.

Follow Quilt Top Assembly diagram to join 2 (2½" x 23½") strips with 1 (2½") square between them. Repeat for 1 more border strip. Join these strips to sides of quilt.

Join 2 (2½" x 17½") strips with 3 (2½") squares as shown in diagram for top border. Repeat for bottom border. Join borders to top and bottom of quilt.

5. Layer batting; top, right side up; and backing, right side down. Baste. With batting against feed dogs, machine-stitch around edges, leaving a 12" opening. Turn through opening. Slipstitch opening closed.

6. Outline-quilt all Evening Star block pieces. Follow design to quilt preprinted blocks.

Block 1

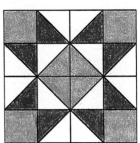

Block 2

Quilt Top Assembly

On Christmas Eve, 1822, Dr. Clement C. Moore penned the lines illustrated in this bright wall hanging. The poem, "The Night Before Christmas," was written as a special gift for Moore's six-year-old daughter, Charity.

Fan Sampler

Setting large pieces of print fabric together with just a few pieced blocks cuts piecing time considerably. The large rectangles of background fabric comprise more than two-thirds of this quilt top's total area. But the eight fan blocks, pieced in striking tones of solid colors, blend so well with the background print that this beautiful quilt looks anything but quick-pieced.

Finished Sizes
Quilt: 46″ x 52″
Blocks: 8 (8″) Fan Blocks

Fabrics

Floral print	1 5/8 yards
6 coordinating solids	1/4 yard each
White	5/8 yard
Backing	3 1/8 yards
Coordinating fabric for binding	1/2 yard

Instructions

1. Cut floral print into 3 (10½″ x 52½″) strips and 10 (4½″ x 8½″) rectangles. Set aside.

2. From white fabric, cut 8 (8½″) squares. Set aside.

3. Use templates on pages 82 and 83 to cut remaining pieces, following instructions on templates.

4. Follow block diagrams to make 8 fan blocks as follows: First piece fan blades. Join blades to corner wedge (piece A or B). (See instructions for sewing curves, page 8.) Clip curves along top of fan. Pin fan in place on 1 white square. Turn under edges along top of fan and appliqué by hand to white square. Repeat for remaining blocks.

(*Note:* When making Block 2, first make fan from B and E pieces. Then appliqué fan to piece D before appliquéing to white square.)

5. Trim background (white square) from behind fans, leaving ¼″ seam allowances.

6. Follow Quilt Top Assembly diagram to set blocks together with 4½″ x 8½″ rectangles to form 2 vertical rows.

7. Machine-quilt each vertical row, including long print strips, as follows: Quilt long print strips with 4 vertical rows at 2″ intervals as shown in Quilt Top Assembly diagram. Quilt fans in-the-ditch of all seams.

8. Follow Quilt Top Assembly diagram to join quilted vertical rows. (See *Heart's Desire*, Step 7, page 72, to join rows.)

9. Bind with bias binding. (See Binding Your Quilt, page 89.)

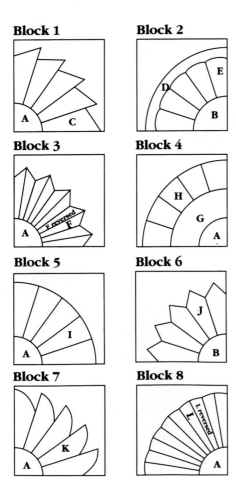

Quilt Top Assembly

*E*ight fan blocks on a
floral background give this wall
quilt an oriental flair. The vertical rows
are machine-quilted, then joined.

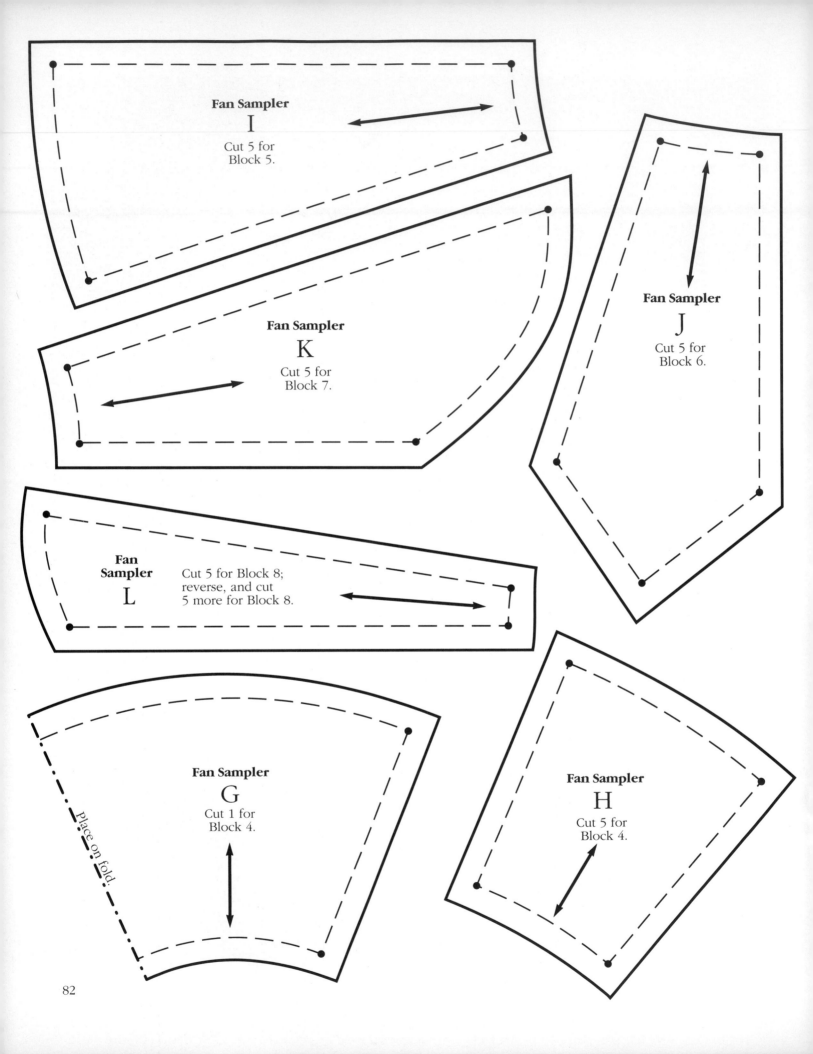

Fan Sampler
I

Cut 5 for
Block 5.

Fan Sampler
K

Cut 5 for
Block 7.

Fan Sampler
J

Cut 5 for
Block 6.

Fan Sampler
L

Cut 5 for Block 8;
reverse, and cut
5 more for Block 8.

Fan Sampler
G

Cut 1 for
Block 4.

Place on fold.

Fan Sampler
H

Cut 5 for
Block 4.

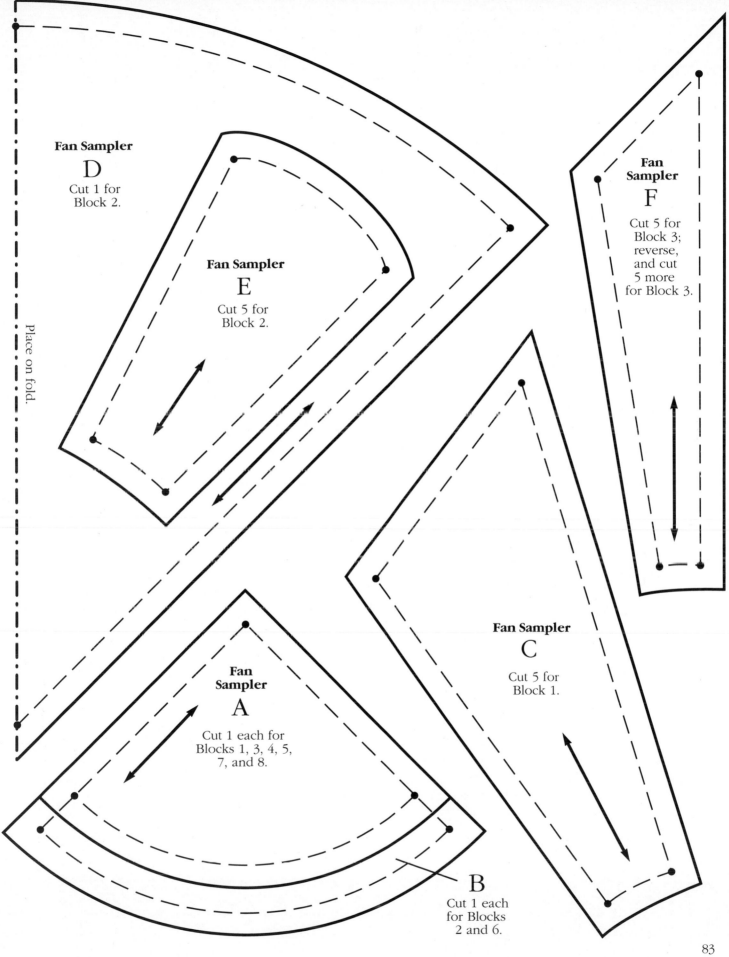

Fan Sampler

D

Cut 1 for
Block 2.

Place on fold.

Fan Sampler

E

Cut 5 for
Block 2.

Fan Sampler

F

Cut 5 for
Block 3;
reverse,
and cut
5 more
for Block 3.

Fan Sampler

C

Cut 5 for
Block 1.

**Fan
Sampler**

A

Cut 1 each for
Blocks 1, 3, 4, 5,
7, and 8.

B

Cut 1 each
for Blocks
2 and 6.

Instant Patchwork "Quillow"

Folded and placed inside its matching zippered cover, this lightweight lap quilt becomes a pillow. Three coordinating prints were used to make this project. The pillow cover is made from two preprinted quilt blocks and lined with coordinating miniprint. The quilt top, which looks as if it is made from tiny fabric scraps, is actually one piece of patchwork print. It is backed with the same coordinating miniprint that lines the pillow.

Finished Sizes
Quilt: 42″ x 42″
Pillow Cover: 16″ x 16″

Fabrics and Materials
2 preprinted quilt blocks (at least
  16½″ square)
Coordinating
  miniprint   1¾ yards
Coordinating
  patchwork print   1¼ yards
Batting: 1 (42½″) square, 2 (16½″)
  squares
14″ zipper
Matching embroidery floss

Instructions

1. Trim preprinted blocks to measure 16½″ square. Cut miniprint into 2 (16½″) squares and 1 (42½″) square. Cut patchwork print into 1 (42½″) square.

2. Make pillow as follows: Layer 1 block, right side down; 1 (16½″) square of batting; and 1 (16½″) square of miniprint, right side up. Baste around all sides. Repeat for second block. Hand- or machine-quilt blocks as desired, following design. Trim batting from seam allowances.

Determine on which side zipper is to be placed. With block sides facing and raw edges aligned, machine-baste blocks together along this side. Press seam open. Center zipper on back of seam and insert zipper according to package instructions. Unzip zipper.

With right sides facing, stitch from 1 end of zipper around other 3 sides of pillow, ending at other end of zipper. Turn pillow through opening.

3. Make quilt as follows: Layer batting; patchwork print square, right side up; 42½″ miniprint square, right side down. Baste. With batting against feed dogs, join sides of quilt, leaving a 12″ opening on 1 side. Turn through opening. Slipstitch opening closed.

Cut embroidery floss into 2″ lengths and tie quilt through all layers at regular intervals as desired.

4. To place quilt inside pillow cover, fold quilt into thirds lengthwise. Then fold into thirds crosswise. Insert in pillow cover.

Using preprinted patchwork you can finish this lap quilt and pillow cover in a day. It makes a handy take-along for picnics or sports events.

Tic-Tac-Toe

Using striped fabric in patchwork can give you a strip-pieced look without spending the time it takes to strip piece. If time is no object, try strip-piecing solid or print fabric into 6½″ striped squares and cutting the B pieces from them.

The quilt is the right size for lap or crib. The pillow is made from one X block and one O block, joined and bordered by a four-inch ruffle.

X Block

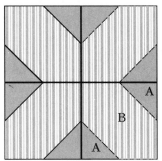

O Block

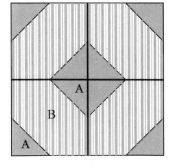

QUILT

Finished Sizes
Quilt: 44″ x 44″ (excluding ruffle)
Blocks: 5 (12″) X Blocks
4 (12″) O Blocks

Fabrics
Dk. pink solid	2½ yards
Pink stripe	1¼ yards
Backing	2¾ yards

Instructions
1. Use templates on page 88 to cut A and B pieces as indicated or see Quick Tip on page 88.
2. Refer to block diagrams below to piece 5 X blocks and 4 O blocks.
3. From pink solid, cut 6 (2½″ x 12½″) sashing strips. Join blocks with sashing strips to form 3 horizontal rows of 3 blocks each (see photograph). From pink solid, cut 2 (2½″ x 40½″) sashing strips. Join rows with strips as shown in photograph. Cut 4 (2½″-wide) border strips from pink solid and join to quilt as shown in photograph.
4. From pink solid, cut and piece a 4½″ x 264″ strip for ruffle. Join ends of strip to form continuous strip. With wrong sides facing and raw edges aligned, fold strip in half lengthwise and press. Gather raw edge to fit perimeter of quilt. With raw edges aligned, baste ruffle to quilt top.
5. With ruffle toward center of quilt, layer batting; top, right side up; and backing, right side down. Baste. With batting against feed dogs, join edges of quilt, leaving a 12″ opening on 1 side. Turn through opening. Slipstitch opening closed.
6. Machine-quilt in-the-ditch around each X and O.

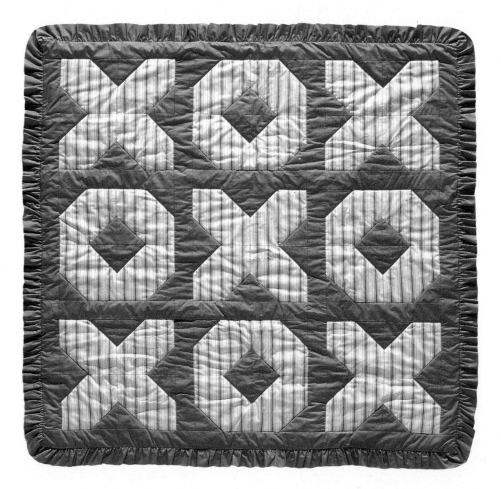

PILLOW

Finished Sizes
Pillow: 16" x 16" (excluding ruffle)
Blocks: 1 (12") X Block
       1 (12") O Block

Fabrics and Materials
Dk. pink solid   ¾ yard
Pink stripe   ½ yard
Backing   ½ yard
2 (16½") squares of batting
Polyester stuffing

Instructions

1. Cut A and B pieces as indicated on templates below or see Quick Tip below.

2. See block diagrams on page 86 to piece 1 X block and 1 O block.

3. Cut 2 (2½" x 12½") strips from solid pink and join to top and bottom of X block. Cut 2 (2½" x 16½") strips from pink solid and join to sides of block. Repeat for O block.

4. Cut backing fabric into 2 (16½") squares. Stack 1 backing square, right side down; batting; and 1 block, right side up. Baste. Machine-quilt in-the-ditch around striped pieces. Trim batting from seam. Repeat for remaining block.

5. From pink solid, cut and piece a 4½" x 72" strip for ruffle. Refer to Step 4 of quilt instructions on page 86 to join ruffle to 1 of the pillow blocks.

6. With right sides facing and ruffle toward center of pillow, join blocks, leaving a 6" opening. Turn and stuff pillow. Slipstitch opening closed.

QUICK TIP

For an even quicker method of making the X and O blocks, use the following rotary-cutting instructions instead of templates: Cut half-square triangles from 3⅞" squares to form as many As as needed. (See Making Half-Square and Quarter-Square Triangles, page 5.) To make Bs, cut 1 (6½") square for each B. Use quilter's ruler to cut away 2 diagonally opposite corners 3⅛" from the corner.

Tic-Tac-Toe

B

Cut 36 striped for quilt.
Cut 8 striped for pillow.

Tic-Tac-Toe

A

Cut 72 solid for quilt.
Cut 16 solid for pillow.

Binding Your Quilt

The quickest and easiest way to bind your quilt is to use purchased bias binding. But color choices are limited and many quilts need custom-made binding.

To determine the length of binding needed, add the length and width of your quilt and multiply by 2 to get the perimeter in inches. Add 10″ for corner overlaps. To get the number of yards, divide by 36″.

Straight-Grain Binding

To determine the amount of fabric needed to make straight-grain binding, divide the number of inches of binding needed by 42″ (the average width of fabric after shrinkage). Multiply that number by the desired width of binding (usually 2½″).

Mark off your fabric in horizontal lines the width of the binding. (See Diagram 1, Figure 1.) With right sides facing, fold the fabric in half, offsetting drawn lines by matching letters and matching raw edges as shown in Diagram 1, Figure 2. Join. Cut the binding in a continuous strip, starting with the protruding point and following the marked lines around the tube. Fold the strip in half lengthwise and press it.

Diagram 1: Making Continuous Straight-Grain Binding

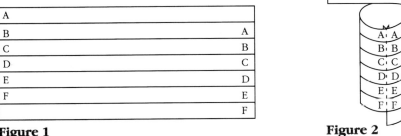

Figure 1   **Figure 2**

Continuous Bias Binding

To make continuous bias binding, you'll need a square of fabric. Multiply the number of inches of binding needed by the desired width of binding. Find the square root of that number. (A calculator with a square-root function is helpful here.) That's the size of the square needed to make your binding.

Cut the square in half diagonally to form 2 triangles. With right sides facing, join the triangles as shown in Diagram 2, Figure 1. Press the seam open. Mark off parallel lines the desired width of the binding. (See Diagram 2, Figure 2.) With right sides facing, align the raw edges marked Seam 2. As you align the edges, extend a Seam 2 point past its natural matching point by the distance of the width of the bias strip. Join. Cut the binding in a continuous strip, starting with the protruding point and following the marked lines around the tube. (See Diagram 2, Figure 3.) Fold the strip in half lengthwise and press it.

Diagram 2: Making Continuous Bias Binding

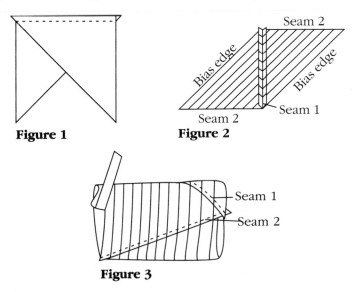

Figure 1   **Figure 2**

Figure 3

CHAPTER FIVE

• • •

A t times my head fills with dusty sweet memories of my Maw Maw's small farm. I recall the crunchy Jerusalem artichokes that grew in her backyard, the pie safe in the kitchen that smelled like cinnamon, a flock of marauding geese that terrified me, the horseshoe nailed above the front door (with its open end up to hold the good luck), a mulberry tree, a log barn, and so much more.

Maw Maw's life was a routine, with everything done at a particular time for a particular reason. When I spent the night with her, hair (hers and mine) was always brushed and braided before breakfast; hands were always washed (with her strong homemade soap) before meals; and during a thunderstorm, under Maw Maw's orders everyone always retired to the storm cellar, a place whose mere mention would send me hiding under the kitchen table.

It was one of Maw Maw's habits that on a certain day near the onset of winter, but while the weather was still warm and sunny, she would bring out all her winter quilts for washing and drying.

Those quilts seemed to have no kinship with the bright patterned ones that my mother and her friends made. Maw Maw's quilts were heavy, serviceable covers, made from dark wool strips and tied at intervals with strong red yarn. When I lay under a stack of them, their weight was uncomfortable and they scratched my skin. And they always smelled of wood fire and my Paw Paw.

STRIPS
AND
STRINGS

Just look
what you can do us-
ing the time-honored
techniques of strip
piecing and string
piecing!

Finished Sizes

Quilt: 72″ x 92″
Blocks: 12 (20″) Rocky Road to
    Kansas Blocks

Fabrics

Navy solid	5 yards
Assorted solids	6¾ yards
Backing	5½ yards

Instructions

1. Enlarge template patterns on page 94. (See Enlarging Patterns, page 35.)

2. Use Template B to cut 48 pieces from assorted solids. Use Template C to cut 96 pieces from navy.

3. Cut remainder of assorted solids into crosswise strips in assorted widths ranging from 1″ to 2″.

4. (*Note:* Because you have cut the Bs from the same fabric as your crosswise strips, some strips will be longer than others. Start piecing with the longest strips.) Join as many strips as needed along long edges to form a 14″-wide band. Press seams toward darker fabrics. Use template A to cut strip-pieced triangles from this band, staggering triangles across width of band for variety. (See Cutting Triangle

A diagram.) Cut remaining pieced fabric crosswise into 1½″-wide strips. Join these strips end to end to form a long multi-colored strip to incorporate into the next pieced band.

5. Make another pieced band as in Step 4, substituting the multi-colored strip that you just made for 1 of the long solid strips. Trim excess multi-colored strip from edge of band and set aside. Cut strip-pieced triangles. Cut remainder of band into multi-colored strips and join end to end as before. Repeat until you have cut 48 strip-pieced triangle As.

6. Follow Block Assembly diagram to make 12 blocks.

7. Follow Quilt Top Assembly diagram to join blocks in 4 horizontal rows of 3 blocks each. Join rows.

8. From navy, cut 2 (6½″-wide) borders and join to sides of quilt; cut 2 (6½″-wide) borders and join to top and bottom of quilt.

9. Quilt as desired.

10. Join remaining 1½″-wide multi-colored strips end to end to make approximately 9¼ yards of binding. (Piece more bands and cut more 1½″-wide strips if needed.) Bind quilt.

Rock Star

Bright colors on a dark background give this quilt's design a sense of movement as patterns merge and change. The star points are cut from strip-pieced bands. Left-over bands are cut and pieced into multi-colored binding for a stellar finishing touch.

Quilt Top Assembly

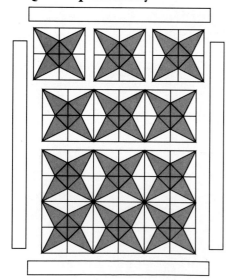

Cutting Triangle A

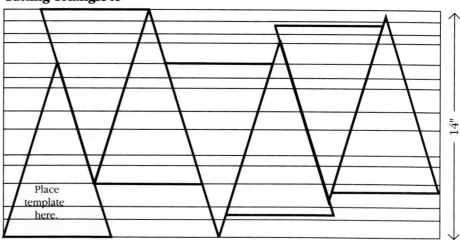

Place template here.

14″

Block Assembly

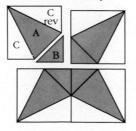

C rev
A
C
B

Rock Star Templates
1 square=½".
Enlarge 200%.

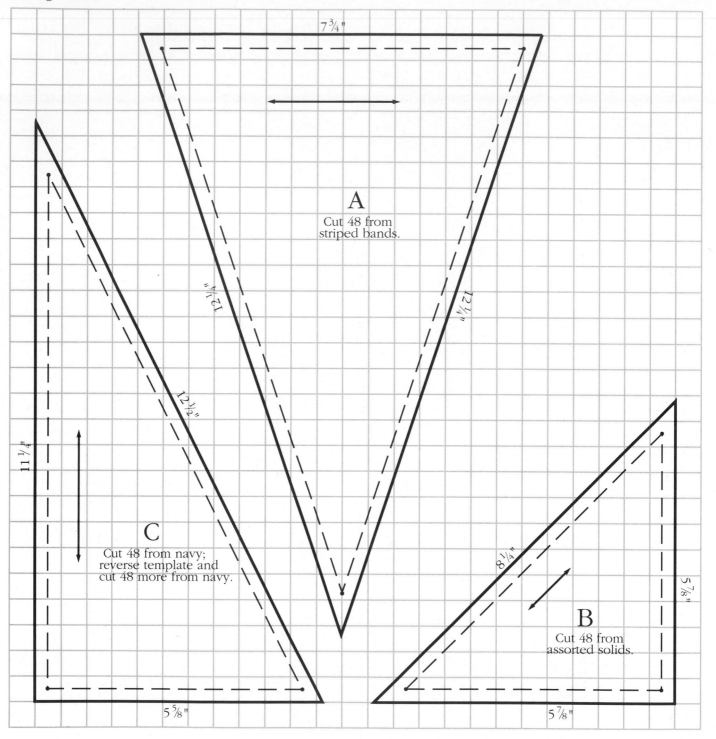

7¾"

A
Cut 48 from
striped bands.

12¼"

12¼"

12½"

11¼"

C
Cut 48 from navy;
reverse template and
cut 48 more from navy.

5⅝"

8¼"

5⅞"

B
Cut 48 from
assorted solids.

5⅞"

Lone Star

The traditional method of making this type of medallion quilt is to use a template to cut each diamond shape and then hand-piece the diamonds into star points. The quick-piecing method here will save you an enormous amount of time and, with careful cutting and sewing, will yield a star whose points fit together perfectly.

The matching pillow shams work up quickly to add the finishing touch to your bed.

Finished Sizes
Quilt: 83″ x 92″
Pillow Shams: 20½″ x 26½″
  (excluding ruffle)

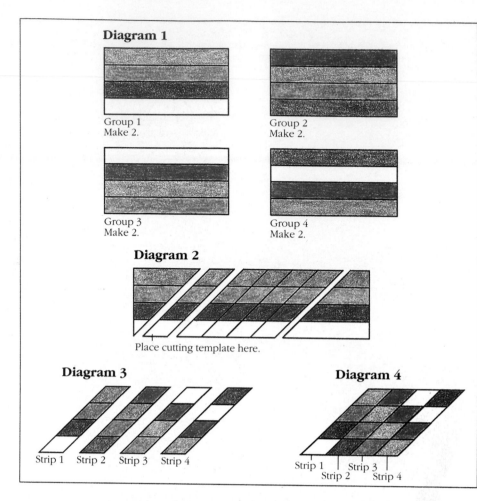

Diagram 1

Group 1
Make 2.

Group 2
Make 2.

Group 3
Make 2.

Group 4
Make 2.

Diagram 2

Place cutting template here.

Diagram 3

Strip 1   Strip 2   Strip 3   Strip 4

Diagram 4

Strip 1   Strip 3
Strip 2   Strip 4

Quilt Top Assembly

B   A
C

QUILT

Fabrics

Blue print #1	1⅛ yards
Blue print #2	⅞ yard
Rose print #1	⅞ yard
Rose print #2	⅞ yard
Lt. print	⅞ yard
Blue print for background	2⅛ yards
Rose print for inner border	2 yards
Blue print for outer border	2⅞ yards
Backing	6 yards
Rose print for bias binding	1 yard

Instructions

1. Cut first 5 fabrics into 3½″-wide crosswise strips. Join strips according to Diagram 1. Using cutting template on page 99, cut pieced bands into diagonal strips as shown in Diagram 2.

Join diagonal strips as shown in Diagrams 3 and 4 to form star point. Repeat to make 8 star points. Set aside.

2. From blue print background fabric, cut 4 (19⅞″) squares and 1 (25¼″) square. Cut 19⅞″ squares in half diagonally to form 8 half-square triangles (piece A on Quilt Top Assembly diagram). (See Making Half-Square and Quarter-Square Triangles, page 5.) Cut 25¼″ square into quarters diagonally to form 4 quarter-square triangles (piece B on Quilt Top Assembly diagram). From remainder of blue background fabric, cut 4 (2″ x 24½″) strips (piece C on Quilt Top Assembly diagram).

3. Following Quilt Top Assembly diagram, join star points with pieces A, B, and C to form center medallion.

4. From rose print, cut 2 (3½″-wide) border strips and join to sides of quilt. Cut 2 (3½″-wide) border strips and join to top and bottom of quilt.

5. From blue print, cut 2 (13″-wide) border strips and join to top and bottom of quilt. Cut 2 (8½″-wide) border strips and join to sides of quilt.

6. Machine-quilt in-the-ditch or as desired. Bind with continuous bias binding made from rose print. (See Binding Your Quilt, page 89.)

PILLOW SHAMS

Fabrics and Materials

Blue print #1	⅛ yard
Blue print #2	⅛ yard
Rose print	⅛ yard
Lt. print	⅛ yard
Blue pindot	1⅝ yards
Lt. print for ruffle	2½ yards
2 standard pillows	

Instructions

1. Cut star points from first 4 fabrics as indicated on template.

2. From blue pindot, cut 2 (21″ x 26¾″) rectangles and 4 (15″ x 21″) rectangles.

3. Cut ruffle fabric into 10 (8½″-wide) crosswise strips.

4. Follow Pillow Sham Star diagram on page 99 and photograph to make 1 (8-pointed) star from star points.

5. Press under ¼″ along raw edges of star. Center and baste star in place on right side of 1 (21″ x 26¾″) rectangle. Topstitch in place near edge of star.

6. Join ends of 5 ruffle strips to make 1 long strip. Join ends of strip to make continuous strip. With wrong sides facing and raw edges aligned, fold fabric in half lengthwise and

press entire length of strip.

Gather raw edge of ruffle to fit perimeter of pillow sham top. With raw edges aligned, baste ruffle to right side of sham top.

7. To make sham back, narrowly hem 1 (21″) edge of each of 2 (15″ x 21″) rectangles. With right sides facing, raw edges aligned, and ruffle to-

ward center, pin rectangles to sham top so that hemmed edges overlap at the center of sham. Join back pieces to sham top with ¼″ seam. Turn through opening in center back. Insert standard pillow.

Repeat Steps 4–7 to make second pillow sham.

Pillow Sham Star Template

For each sham, cut 2 each from rose print #1, lt. print, blue print #1, and blue print #2.

Pillow Sham Star

●○

●✕

Lone Star Cutting Template

Trace template, transferring markings.
Turn paper with tracing upside down.
Match X on tracing paper to O on pattern
and O on tracing paper to X on pattern.
Trace pattern again to complete template.

Completed cutting template
should look like this.

Seminole Patchwork

This colorful form of strip piecing originated with Seminole women of south Florida around the end of the 19th century. Many of the patterns and designs have been handed down from generation to generation and are symbolic of forms in nature. Some designs represent the families who developed them. The technique makes perfect use of your rotary-cutting equipment and skills.

On the following pages, you will find diagrams and instructions for five Seminole patchwork designs. The bands can be used to make quilts, pillows, and wall hangings; or they can be added as accents to vests, jackets, skirts, and tote bags.

Measurements on diagrams indicate cut sizes, *not* finished sizes.

FAMILY

Finished Size
Band: Approximately 1⅜ yards long

Fabrics
Yellow, blue, dk. red, purple, green, and lt. red   ⅛ yard each

Instructions

1. Cut 1 (1½"-wide) crosswise strip each from yellow and lt. red. Cut 1 (1¼"-wide) crosswise strip from each of remaining fabrics. Join strips along long edges as shown in Diagram 1, Figure 1, with yellow at top and lt. red at bottom. Cut across pieced band at 1¼" intervals as shown.

Rearrange units side by side, with pattern offset down as shown in Figure 2. Match seams and join.

2. Join band to foundation fabric across top and bottom as shown in Figure 3.

The bright geometric patterns on the jacket and vest are examples of Native American patchwork art.

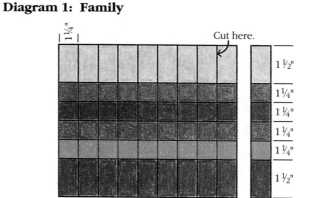

Diagram 1: Family

1¼"

Cut here.

1½"
1¼"
1¼"
1¼"
1¼"
1½"

Figure 1

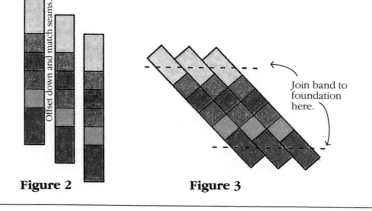

Offset down and match seams.

Join band to foundation here.

Figure 2   **Figure 3**

Diagram 2: Sacred Fire

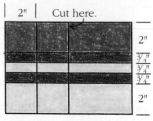

Figure 1: Band A (Make 2.)

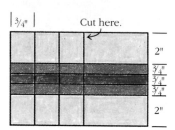

Figure 2: Band B

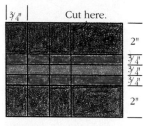

Figure 3: Band C

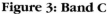
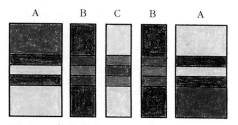

Figure 4: Joining Bands

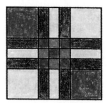

Figure 5: Sacred Fire Block

SACRED FIRE

Finished Size
Blocks: 21 (3¾″) Sacred Fire blocks
Band: Approximately 3 yards long

Fabrics

Red	¾ yard
Brown	¼ yard
Yellow	⅜ yard
Blue	⅛ yard

Instructions

1. From red fabric, cut 2 (2″-wide) and 3 (¾″-wide) crosswise strips. From brown, cut 2 (2″-wide) and 4 (¾″-wide) crosswise strips. From yellow, cut 4 (2″-wide) and 2 (¾″-wide) crosswise strips. From blue, cut 3 (¾″-wide) crosswise strips.

Join strips along long edges as shown in Diagram 2, Figures 1, 2, and 3 to make 2 Band As, 1 Band B, and 1 Band C. Cut across bands at indicated intervals.

Follow Figure 4 to join sections of the 3 bands to make 1 Sacred Fire block. (See Figure 5 for completed block.)

Repeat Step 1 until all units are made into blocks.

2. From remaining red fabric, cut 1 (4¼″-wide) crosswise strip. Cut across strip at 5″ intervals as shown in Diagram 3, Figure 1.

Join red rectangles with Sacred Fire blocks as shown in Figure 2.

Following Figure 3, measure 1″ from left edge on bottom of pieced row. With 45° line of quilter's ruler aligned with bottom edge of pieced row, cut from 1″ mark across red rectangle. Measure ¾″ from right edge on bottom of first Sacred Fire block. With 45° line aligned with bottom of row, cut from ¾″ mark across rectangle. Continue making cuts in same manner across row as shown.

Rearrange units side by side, with pattern offset down as shown in Figure 4. Match seams and join.

3. Join band to foundation fabric across top and bottom as shown in Diagram 3, Figure 5.

*J*ust as early American women gave names to their quilt patterns based on nature, religion, or events of the day, Seminole women named their patchwork designs after their own experiences and dreams. From top to bottom, the designs that embellish this vest are Trail of Tears, Diamonds, Tiger Teeth, and Sacred Fire. The designs are joined by solid fabric strips in varying widths.

Diagram 3: Joining Sacred Fire Blocks

|← 5" →| Cut here.

4 ¼"

Figure 1

Figure 2

Cut here.
1" 45° ¾" ¼"

Figure 3

Offset down and match seams.

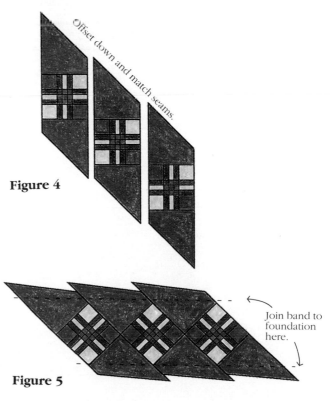

Figure 4

Join band to foundation here.

Figure 5

TIGER TEETH

Finished Size
Band: Approximately ¾ yard long

Fabrics

Red	¼ yard
White	⅛ yard
Navy	⅛ yard

Instructions

1. From red fabric, cut 2 (2½″-wide) crosswise strips. From white, cut 1 (¾″-wide) crosswise strip. From navy, cut 1 (1½″-wide) crosswise strip. Join strips along long edges as shown in Diagram 4, Figure 1.

2. With 45° line on quilter's ruler aligned with top edge of pieced band, cut across band at 45° angle at 2″ intervals as shown in Figure 2.

3. Rearrange units side by side, with pattern offset up as shown in Figure 3. Match seams and join.

4. Join band to foundation fabric across top and bottom as shown in Figure 4.

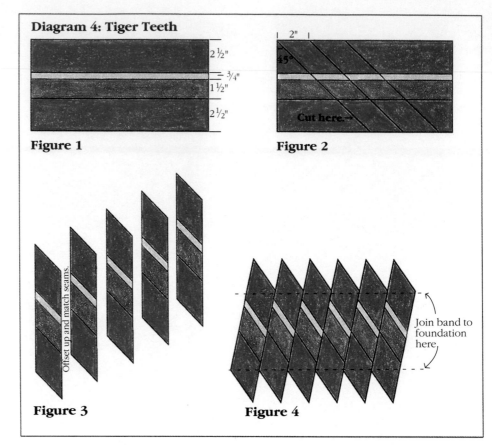

Diagram 4: Tiger Teeth

Figure 1

Figure 2

Figure 3

Figure 4

DIAMONDS

Finished Size
Band: Approximately ½ yard long

Fabrics
White, yellow, orange, lt. red, dk. red ⅛ yard each

Instructions

1. Cut 1 (1½″-wide) crosswise strip each from white and dk. red fabrics. Cut 1 (1¼″-wide) crosswise strip each from remaining fabrics. Join strips along long edge as shown in Diagram 5, Figure 1.

2. With 45° line on quilter's ruler aligned with bottom edge of pieced band, cut across band at 45° angle at 2″ intervals as shown in Figure 2.

3. Rearrange units side by side, with pattern offset up as shown in Figure 3. Match seams and join.

4. Join band to foundation fabric across top and bottom as shown in Figure 4.

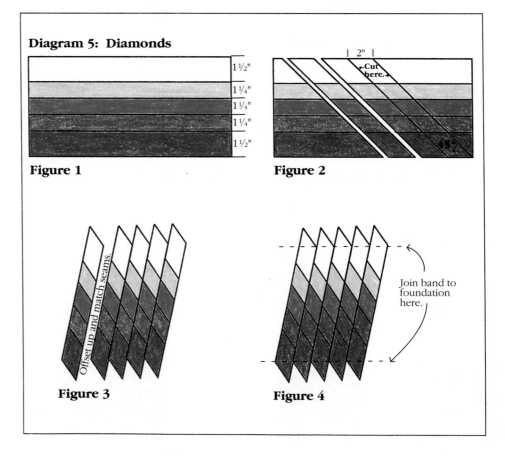

Diagram 5: Diamonds

Figure 1

Figure 2

Figure 3

Figure 4

TRAIL OF TEARS

Finished Size
Band: Approximately 1 yard long

Fabrics
Turquoise, terra-
cotta, gold, and
navy   ⅛ yard each

Instructions

1. Cut 1 (3″-wide) crosswise strip each from turquoise and navy fabrics. Cut 1 (¾″-wide) crosswise strip from terra-cotta fabric. Cut 1 (1¼″-wide) crosswise strip from gold fabric. Join strips along long edge as shown in Diagram 6, Figure 1.

2. With 45° line on quilter's ruler aligned with bottom edge of pieced band, cut across band at 45° angle at 2″ intervals as shown in Figure 2.

3. Rearrange units side by side, with pattern offset up as shown in Figure 3. Match seams and join.

4. Join band to foundation fabric across top and bottom as shown in Figure 4.

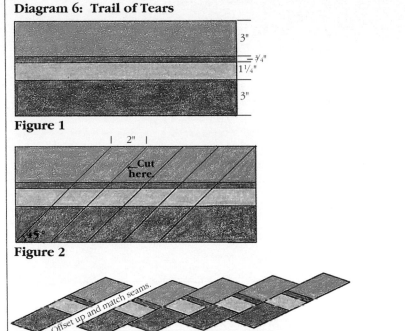

Diagram 6: Trail of Tears

3″
¾″
1¼″
3″

Figure 1

| 2″ |

Cut here.

45°

Figure 2

Offset up and match seams.

Figure 3

Join band to foundation here.

Figure 4

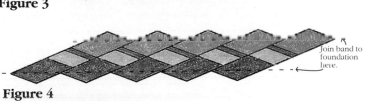

The front of this denim jacket is emblazoned with a Seminole design known as Family. Additional strips of fabric and lengths of rickrack have been added to the top and bottom of each multi-colored band.

105

Log Cabin Variation

Follow the diagrams carefully for an easy-piecing solution to this interesting variation on the very popular Log Cabin theme.

Finished Sizes
Quilt: 84" x 104"
Blocks: 32 (12") Log Cabin Blocks
  14 Half-Blocks
  4 Quarter-Blocks

Fabrics
Navy solid	3½ yards
Pink solid	½ yard
Assorted lt. and med. prints	5½ yards
Backing	6 yards
Navy for binding	1 yard

Instructions

1. Cut 4 (2½"-wide) lengthwise strips from navy. Set strips aside for borders.

Cut remainder of navy, pink, and prints into 2½"-wide crosswise strips.

2. Join long edges of 1 navy strip and 1 pink strip. Repeat to make 5 more navy/pink bands. Cut across bands at 2½" intervals to make 96 navy/pink units. (See Diagram 1.)

Cut across remaining pink strip at 2½" intervals to make 14 A squares.

3. Cut across print strips at 2½" intervals to make 160 A squares. Cut across remaining print strips to make 320 (2½" x 4½") B rectangles and 160 (2½" x 6½") C rectangles.

4. Follow Diagram 2 to make 1 block. Repeat to make 32 blocks.

5. Follow Diagram 3 on page 108 to make 1 half-block. Repeat to make a total of 14 half-blocks.

Diagram 1

2½" | Cut here.

					Pink
					Navy

Diagram 2

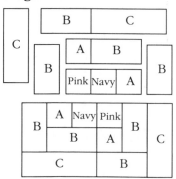

Place quilter's ruler over 1 half-block as shown in Diagram 4, having ¼″ line covering points where squares meet (dots on Diagram). With rotary cutter, trim points of squares and rectangles as shown. Repeat for remaining half-blocks.

6. Follow Diagram 5 to make 1 quarter-block. Repeat to make 4 quarter-blocks. Trim points on both sides as shown in Step 5. (See Diagram 6.)

7. Using remaining navy strips for sashing, join blocks, half-blocks, and quarter-blocks with sashing strips in diagonal rows as shown in Quilt Top Assembly diagram. Join rows. Join borders to quilt, trimming strips to fit and mitering corners.

8. Quilt in-the-ditch of all seams. Bind with continuous bias binding made from navy fabric. (See Binding Your Quilt, page 89.)

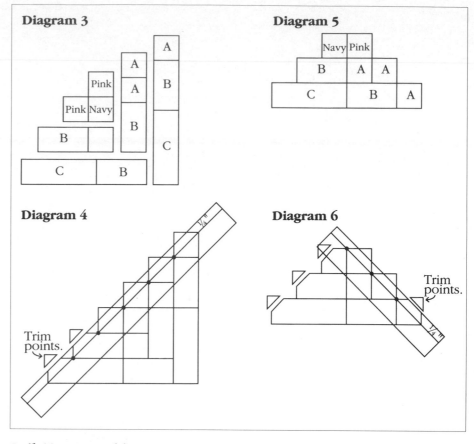

Quilt Top Assembly

Double Irish Chain

The chain effect in this traditional beauty is achieved by the
alternate placement of two easy
strip-pieced blocks. When finished,
the block division is not apparent.

Finished Sizes
Quilt: 84″ x 104″
Blocks: 32 (10″) Block As
31 (10″) Block Bs

Fabrics
Rose print	1⅜ yards
Green print	2½ yards
Muslin	3¼ yards
Narrow inner border	½ yard
Wide outer border	2 yards
Backing	6¼ yards
Rose print for bias binding	1 yard

Instructions

1. Cut rose print into 18 (2½″-wide) crosswise strips. From green print, cut 24 (2½″-wide) crosswise strips. From muslin, cut 8 (2½″-wide) crosswise strips. Join strips according to Diagram 1.

Cut across pieced bands at 2½″ intervals to form pieced units. Assemble block with pieced units as shown in Diagram 2. Repeat to make a total of 32 Block As.

2. From muslin, cut 12 (6½″-wide) crosswise strips. Cut across 8 of these strips at 10½″ intervals to form 31 (6½″ x 10½″) rectangles. Set aside.

From remaining green print, cut 8 (2½″-wide) crosswise strips. Join green strips with remaining 4 muslin strips according to Diagram 3.

Cut across pieced bands at 2½″ intervals to form pieced units. Join 1 (6½″ x 10½″) muslin rectangle and 2 pieced units as shown in Diagram 4 to make 1 Block B. Repeat to make 31 Block Bs.

3. Follow Quilt Top Assembly diagram to join blocks in 9 horizontal rows of 7 blocks each. Join rows.

4. From inner border fabric, cut 8 (1½″-wide) crosswise strips. Piece where necessary to make borders and

Diagram 1

Group 1
Make 4.

Group 2
Make 4.

Group 3
Make 2.

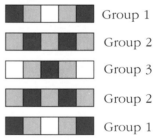

Diagram 2: Block A

Group 1
Group 2
Group 3
Group 2
Group 1

Diagram 3

Width of fabric   2½″ 2½″

Group 4
Make 4.

Diagram 4: Block B

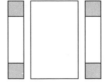

join to quilt as shown in Quilt Top Assembly diagram.

5. From outer border fabric, cut 8 (6½"-wide) crosswise strips. Piece where necessary to make borders and join to quilt as shown in Quilt Top Assembly diagram.

6. Quilt in-the-ditch of rose and green squares. Transfer the quilting pattern (right) to muslin (see photograph) and quilt. (See Machine Quilting, page 9.)

7. Bind with continuous bias binding made from rose print. (See Binding Your Quilt, page 89.)

Block A

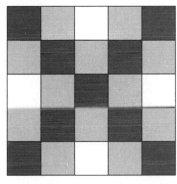

Block B

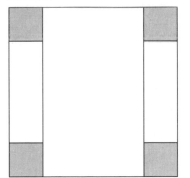

Double Irish Chain Quilting Pattern

Half Pattern
Trace pattern. Reverse at dots and trace other half of pattern.

Quilt Top Assembly

Roaming Stripes

Bold colors highlight this queen-size quilt. Black half-square triangles form the background, giving the quilt an Amish flavor. The striped triangles are cut from multi-colored strip-pieced units.

Finished Sizes
Quilt: 103″ x 113″
Blocks: 90 (10″) Blocks

Fabrics and Materials
Black solid	7¾ yards
Assorted solids	7 yards
Blue solid	3 yards
Backing	10 yards
Black quilting thread	

Instructions
1. Cut 45 (10⅞″) squares from black fabric. Cut squares in half diagonally to make 90 half-square triangles. (See Making Half-Square and Quarter-Square Triangles, page 5.)

2. Cut assorted solids into 115 (2″-wide) crosswise strips. Join 5 strips along long edges. Repeat to make 22 more 5-strip units, alternating color sequence.

Make a triangle template by cutting a 10⅞″ square in half diagonally. Use the template to cut 90 triangles from strip-pieced units. (See Cutting Strip-Pieced Triangles diagram.)

3. Follow Block Assembly diagram to join 1 black triangle to 1 strip-pieced triangle. Repeat to make 89 more blocks.

4. Follow Quilt Top Assembly diagram to join blocks in 10 horizontal rows of 9 blocks each. Join rows.

5. From blue solid, cut 2 (2″-wide) inner border strips and join to top and bottom of quilt. Cut 2 (2″-wide) strips and join to sides of quilt.

6. From black, cut 2 (5½″-wide) outer border strips and join to top and bottom of quilt. Cut 2 (5½″-wide) border strips and join to sides of quilt.

7. With black quilting thread, outline-quilt colored strips. Quilt black triangles as desired.

8. Bind with continuous bias binding made from black fabric. (See Binding Your Quilt, page 89.)

Cutting Strip-Pieced Triangles

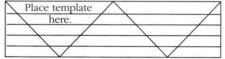

Place template here.

Block Assembly

Quilt Top Assembly

Confetti Toss

Here's a great design for using up all those odd-size scraps of fabric in your scrap bag. This quilt was made by Judyth Gordon Smith's mother, Lillian Ginn Gordon. Lillian's own mother taught her this method of string piecing. The vertical strings were pieced onto two-column-wide strips of newspaper. Scraps in the quilt date from about the 1920s to the 1950s.

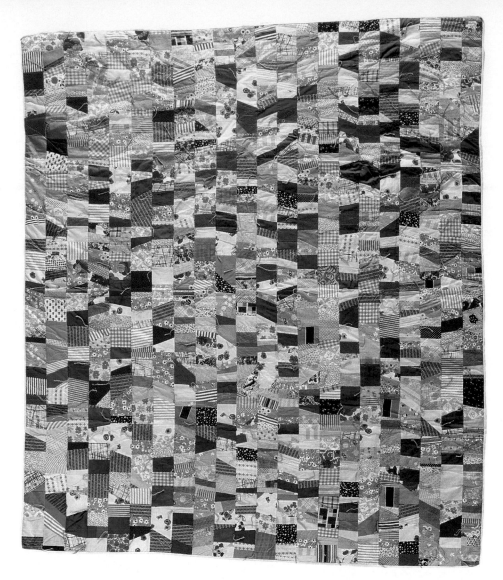

QUICK TIP

You may wish to string-piece your quilt the old fashioned way, using paper as the foundation instead of muslin. If so, I recommend that you *not* use newspaper because the ink can be very messy. Lightweight paper bags, 8½″ x 11″ sheets of white paper, or rolls of plain brown wrapping paper work well. Cut paper into 4″-wide strips the length of your paper. String-piece strips as in Step 3. Tear away paper foundation. Join strips to form 22 (89½″-long) strips. Join strips to make quilt top.

Finished Sizes
Quilt: 77″ x 89″
Pieced Strings: 22 (3½″ x 89″)

Fabrics and Materials
Muslin for
  foundation   7½ yards
Assorted scraps
Backing   5½ yards
Muslin for binding   1 yard
Blue pearl cotton

Instructions
  1. From muslin, cut 22 (4″ x 89½″) foundation strips for your string-pieced units. (See Quick Tip.)
  2. Press scraps if needed.
  3. With wrong side of scrap facing right side of 1 foundation strip, lay 1 scrap across top of strip. Make sure edges of scrap extend at least to edges of foundation. With right sides facing and raw edges aligned, lay another scrap on top of the first. (See String Piecing diagram, Figure 1.) Join through all layers. Fold second scrap forward and press. (See Figure 2.)
  With right sides facing and raw edges aligned, lay a third scrap on top of the second. (See Figure 3.) Join through all layers. Fold third scrap forward and press. (See Figure 4.)
  Continue until entire foundation strip is covered with scraps. (See Figure 5.) Trim edges of scraps even with edges of foundation strip.
  Repeat Step 3 for a total of 22 string-pieced strips.
  4. Join strips along long edges to make quilt top.
  5. Layer backing, right side down; batting; and top, right side up. Baste. Using 2 (6″) strands of pearl cotton, tie quilt at 6″ intervals through all layers.
  6. Bind quilt with a continuous strip of bias binding made from muslin. (See Binding Your Quilt, page 89.)

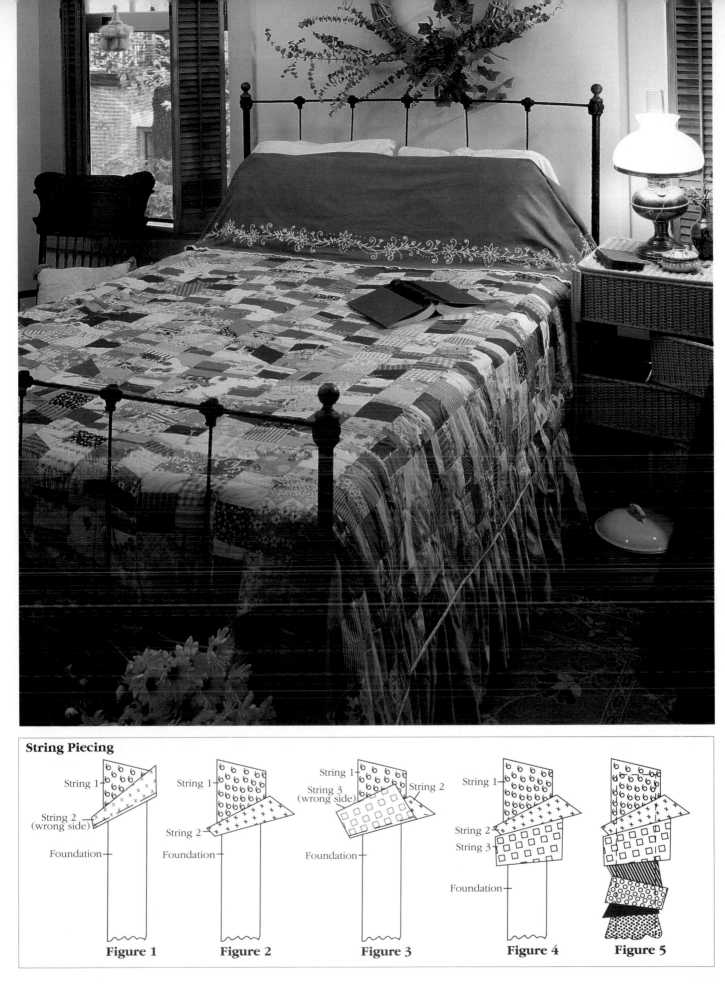

String Piecing

Figure 1

String 1

String 2
(wrong side)

Foundation

Figure 2

String 1

String 2

Foundation

Figure 3

String 1

String 3
(wrong side)

String 2

Foundation

Figure 4

String 1

String 2

String 3

Foundation

Figure 5

• • •

Strange how quilts and soft furry things seem drawn to each other. My cat, Charles, a has-been Tom who, muddy, cold, and homeless, meowed at my door one March evening, is quite partial to quilts. I don't own a quilt that isn't covered with a dusting of gray cat hair. Which reminds me of an incident from my childhood when the warm comfort of an unfinished quilt lulled a wee furry creature into complacent vulnerability.

It was on the occasion of one of many quilting parties held at the home of Mama's friend Marie. Marie's son had a pet flying squirrel, which had the run of the house. The animal loved a crowd and would entertain the ladies by climbing to the top of the living room draperies above the quilting frame and sailing straight down onto the quilt.

One afternoon the quilting group had gathered at Marie's. Several ladies sat around the frame, stitching and talking of people and events of the day. Didn't it look like there would be war in Korea; wasn't Frank Sinatra's music here to stay; and would this fall's fashions include shoulder pads or not?

Suddenly one of the ladies in the group let out a frightened yelp. All eyes lit on her and followed her horrified gaze to a small lump in the quilt between top and backing where her needle had just made a hasty exit—which is exactly what the lump was in the process of doing. A brown blur was seen to hit the floor and dash from the room. After a quick search of the house, Marie found her son's flying squirrel under a bed nursing his back side, which had suffered a vicious jab from the quilter's needle while he napped.

QUICKPATCH FUN

Here's a
scrap bag of tricks
to save you time
and make your quilt-
making sessions
enjoyable, rewarding,
and productive.

Classic Chevrons

The designer of these quilts, Kimberly McKeough, says the pattern is great for those who like to do a lot of fancy quilting. Her piecing method is fast, leaving more time and a perfect canvas to show off quilting stitches.

Try one of the following layouts or design your own quilt, using your imagination and Kimberly's quick-piecing method. (See the cover and page 117 for other views of these quilts.)

ARIZONA SPRING

Finished Size
Quilt: 37″ x 56¼″

Fabrics

Pink solid	1½ yards
Dk. paisley print	1¾ yards
Assorted dk. prints	¾ yard
Assorted lt. prints	¾ yard
Blue print	⅜ yard
Backing	1⅞ yards
Burgundy print for binding	¾ yard

Instructions

1. Cut 4 (1½″-wide) lengthwise strips from pink solid and 4 (3½″-wide) lengthwise strips from paisley. Set aside for borders. Cut a 22″ square from paisley and set aside to make bias binding. Add remaining paisley to assorted dk. prints.

2. Cut lt. and dk. prints into 2″-wide crosswise strips. Cut strips into 84 (2″ x 6″) dk. rectangles and 84 (2″ x 6″) lt. rectangles.

From blue print, cut 2 (8½″) squares. Cut these squares into quarters diagonally to make 8 quarter-square triangles. (See Making Half-Square and Quarter-Square Triangles, page 5.) Set aside 7 of the triangles for use as large triangles. (See Quilt Top Assembly diagram below.) Cut remaining quarter-square triangle in half to make 2 triangles with 6″ bases. Set these aside for use as small triangles. (See Quilt Top Assembly diagram.)

From remaining blue print, cut 44 (2″) squares. From remaining pink solid, cut 40 (2″) squares.

Arizona Spring Quilt Top Assembly

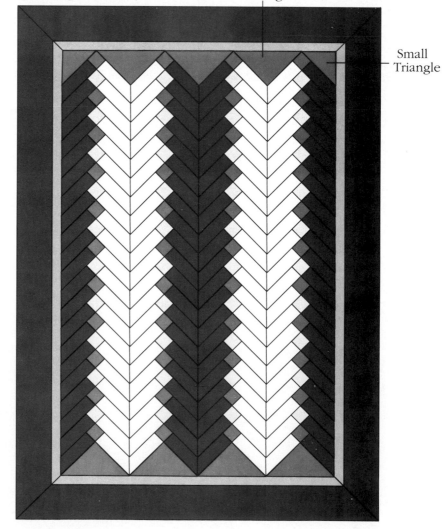

Large Triangle

Small Triangle

118

Shades of blue and burgundy combine to give Arizona Spring *a southwestern look. This quilt is a perfect size to use as a table cover, wall hanging, or other room decoration. (See page 120 for a full view of this quilt.)*

mitering corners. (See Making Borders, page 10.) Join the paisley outer borders to quilt, mitering corners.

9. See photograph for suggested quilting or quilt as desired. Bind with a continuous strip of bias binding made from 22″ paisley square. (See Binding Your Quilt, page 89.)

Diagram 1

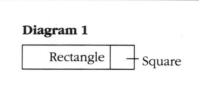

Diagram 2

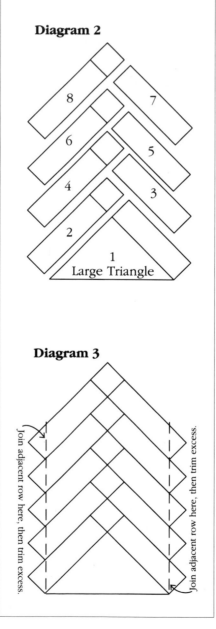

Large Triangle

Diagram 3

Join adjacent row here, then trim excess.

Join adjacent row here, then trim excess.

3. Referring to photograph above for color placement, follow Diagram 1 at right to join 1 (2″) square to 1 (2″ x 6″) rectangle. (*Note:* Square/rectangle strip is on left side of row.) Repeat for a total of 84 square/rectangle strips. (Use chain-piecing method described on page 8 to save time.)

4. Referring to photograph for color placement, make 4 rows of 21 chevrons each, as described in Step 5 below.

5. Following Diagram 2, join 1 rectangle to right side of 1 large triangle (unit 1 in diagram). Join 1 square/ rectangle strip (unit 2 in diagram) to left side of unit 1. Join 1 rectangle (unit 3) to right side of row.

Continue, joining square/rectangle strips to left side and rectangles to right side as shown in diagram until you have built a row of desired number of chevrons.

6. Join rows as shown in Diagram 3 and Quilt Top Assembly diagram. (*Note:* Because rows are all bias-cut and bias edges stretch easily, be very careful and pin frequently when joining sides of rows.)

Trim edges of rows as indicated in Diagram 3.

7. Follow Quilt Top Assembly diagram to join 3 large triangles and 2 small triangles to top of quilt.

8. Join pink inner borders to quilt,

ENGLISH GARDEN

Finished Size
Quilt: 55½″ x 50¾″

Fabrics

Peach floral stripe	1¾ yards
Teal solid	1⅝ yards
Dk. blue print	1½ yards
Assorted blue prints	1 yard
Assorted peach prints	¾ yard
Peach solid	⅛ yard
Rust solid	⅛ yard
Blue solid	⅜ yard

Instructions

1. From peach floral stripe, cut 8 (2½″-wide) lengthwise strips and set aside for sashing and borders. Add remaining floral stripe to assorted peach prints. From teal solid, cut 4 (3¾″-wide) lengthwise strips. Set aside to use as borders. Reserve remaining teal solid to make sashing. From dk. blue print, cut 4 (1¼″-wide) lengthwise strips and set aside for use as borders. Reserve remaining dk. blue print to make binding.

2. Cut assorted blue and peach prints into 2″-wide crosswise strips. Cut blue strips into 144 (2″ x 6″) rectangles. Cut 76 (2″ x 6″) rectangles from peach strips.

From remaining peach strips, cut 45 (2″) squares.

Cut peach solid and rust solid into 2″-wide crosswise strips. Cut peach strips into 40 (2″) squares and rust strips into 10 (2″) squares.

From blue solid, cut 3 (6″) squares and 4 (4¼″) squares. Cut 6″ squares in half diagonally to make 6 half-square triangles. (See Making Half-Square and Quarter-Square Triangles, page 5.) Set aside 5 of these for use as large triangles. (See Quilt Top Assembly diagram, page 121.) Cut the remaining half-square triangle in half to make 2 triangles with 6″ bases. Set these aside for use as small triangles. (See Quilt Top Assembly diagram.) Cut the 4 (4¼″) blue squares in half diagonally to make 8 more small triangles.

3. Referring to photograph, page 121, for color placement, follow Diagram 1 at left to join 1 (2″) square to 1

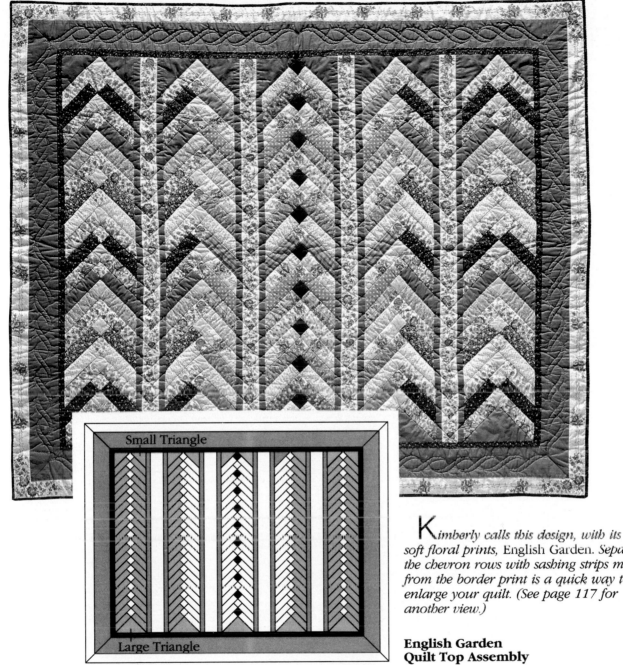

Small Triangle

Large Triangle

*K*imberly calls this design, with its soft floral prints, English Garden. *Separating the chevron rows with sashing strips made from the border print is a quick way to enlarge your quilt. (See page 117 for another view.)*

**English Garden
Quilt Top Assembly**

(2″ x 6″) rectangle. (*Note:* Square/ rectangle strip is on left side of row.) Repeat for a total of 95 square/ rectangle strips. (Use chain-piecing method described on page 8 to save time.)

4. Referring to photograph for color placement, make 5 rows of 19 chevrons each as described in Step 5 of *Arizona Spring* instructions on page 120.

5. Join 1 small triangle to each side at top of each row. (See Quilt Top Assembly diagram.)

6. From remaining teal solid, cut 8 (1¼″ x 50″) lengthwise strips. Trim floral sashing strips to 50″. Join 1 (50″) teal strip to each side of each 50″ floral sashing strip. Follow Quilt Top Assembly diagram and photograph to join chevron rows with pieced sashing strips, trimming sashing to fit rows once joined. (Because rows are all bias-cut and bias edges stretch easily, be very careful and pin frequently when joining sides of rows to sashing.)

7. Mitering corners of all borders,

join dk. blue print borders to quilt; join teal borders to quilt; join floral stripe borders to quilt. (See Making Borders, page 10.)

8. By hand or machine, quilt in-the-ditch of chevrons, extending quilting line into sashing strips. (See photograph.) Quilt teal border with a border quilting design of your choice or with straight lines.

9. Bind with bias binding made from dk. blue print. (See Binding Your Quilt, page 89.)

PRINCESS PRIMROSE PATH

Finished Size
Quilt: 58¼" x 83"

Fabrics

Assorted pale green prints	1½ yards
Assorted pink and rose prints	1 yard
Pale yellow solid	2⅜ yards
Pink solid	¼ yard
Burgundy solid	⅛ yard
Pink floral print	¼ yard
Rose solid	1⅞ yards
Floral stripe	2 yards
Backing	5 yards
Pink solid for binding	⅞ yard

Instructions

1. Cut assorted prints into 2"-wide crosswise strips. Cut green print strips into 162 (2" x 6") rectangles. Cut pink and rose print strips into 108 (2" x 6") rectangles.

From yellow solid, cut 2 (2"-wide) lengthwise strips. From these strips, cut 54 (2") squares.

Cut pink solid into 2"-wide crosswise strips. Cut these pink solid strips into a total of 54 (2") squares.

Cut burgundy solid into 2"-wide crosswise strips. Cut strips into 27 (2") squares.

From pink floral print, cut 3 (8½") squares. Cut squares into quarters diagonally to make 12 quarter-square triangles. (See Making Half-Square and Quarter-Square Triangles, page 5.) Set aside 9 of these triangles for use as large triangles. (See Quilt Top Assembly diagram below.) Cut 1 remaining quarter-square triangle in half to make 2 triangles with 6" bases. Set these aside for use as small triangles. (See Quilt Top Assembly diagram.) (You will have 2 quarter-square triangles remaining to add back to your scrap collection.)

2. Referring to photograph on page 123 for color placement, follow Diagram 1 on page 120 to join 1 (2") square to 1 (2" x 6") rectangle. (*Note:* Square/rectangle strip is on left side of row.) Repeat for a total of 135 square/rectangle strips. (Use chain-piecing method described on page 8 to save time.)

3. Referring to photograph for color placement, make 5 rows of 27 chevrons each as described in Step 5 of *Arizona Spring* instructions on page 120.

4. Follow Step 6 of *Arizona Spring* instructions.

5. Follow Quilt Top Assembly diagram to join 4 large triangles and 2 small triangles to top of quilt.

6. Cut 4 (2"-wide) border strips from rose solid and join to quilt, mitering corners. (See Making Borders, page 10.) Cut 4 (2"-wide) border strips from floral stripe and join to quilt, mitering corners. Cut 4 (8½"-wide) strips from pale yellow and join to quilt, mitering corners.

7. By hand or machine, quilt in-the-ditch of chevrons and inner borders. Use wide outer borders to try out some fancy hand-quilting patterns. Or quilt border with straight diagonal lines as in *Attic Windows*, page 27. Cut flowers from print fabric, adding ¼" seam allowance, and appliqué to outer border as shown in photograph, if desired. (See Quick-Appliqué Techniques, page 58.)

8. Bind quilt with bias binding made from pink solid. (See Binding Your Quilt, page 89.)

Princess Primrose Path
Quilt Top Assembly

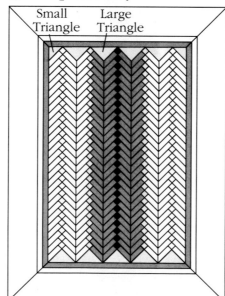

Small Triangle   Large Triangle

Princess Primrose Path *is a wonderful example of how Kimberly McKeough uses print sizes and color values. Says Kimberly, "The key to making this design interesting is using a variety of print sizes—a tiny print next to a large print—and placing light and dark colors side by side." Note how she has appliquéd roses, cut from one of her prints, to the border to enhance the effects of her fancy quilting. (See the cover for another view of this quilt, which Kimberly made for her daughter, Lesleigh.)*

Evening Star

The Evening Star design is an easy one in its own right. And the following quick-cutting and machine-piecing techniques make it even easier and faster.

Finished Sizes
Quilt: 92″ x 104″
Block: 30 (10″) Evening Star Blocks

Fabrics

Dk. blue print	1⅛ yards
Muslin	2⅜ yards
Rose	⅝ yard
Lt. blue print	1⅜ yards
Dk. blue print for border	4¾ yards
Backing	6¼ yards
Muslin for binding	1 yard

Instructions

1. To make triangle As, cut 11 (3⅜″-wide) crosswise strips from dk. blue print. Cut strips into 120 (3⅜″) squares. Cut squares in half diagonally to make 240 half-square triangles. (See Making Half-Square and Quarter-Square Triangles, page 5.)

To make triangle Bs, cut 6 (3⅜″-wide) crosswise strips from muslin. Cut strips into 60 (3⅜″) squares. Cut squares in half diagonally to make 120 half-square triangles.

To make triangle Cs, cut 7 (4⅜″-wide) crosswise strips from muslin. Cut strips into 60 (4⅜″) squares. Cut squares in half diagonally to make 120 half-square triangles.

To make square Ds, cut 10 (3″-wide) crosswise strips from muslin. Cut strips into 120 (3″) squares.

To make square Es, cut 3 (4″-wide) crosswise strips from rose fabric. Cut strips into 30 (4″) squares.

2. Follow Block Assembly diagram to make 30 Evening Star blocks.

Block Assembly

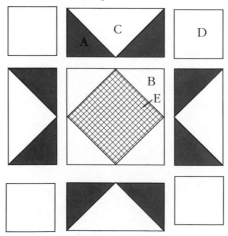

The addition of an extra-wide border gives you a quick way of turning a twin-size quilt into a queen-size quilt.

3. From remaining rose, cut 42 (2½″) sashing squares. From lt. blue print, cut 71 sashing strips as follows: Cut 18 (2½″-wide) crosswise strips. Cut strips into 2½″ x 10½″ strips.

4. Join blocks with sashing strips in 6 horizontal rows of 5 blocks each. Make 7 pieced sashing strips as follows: Join 6 sashing squares with 5 sashing strips as shown in photograph. Join rows with pieced sashing strips as shown.

5. From border fabric, cut 2 (15½″-wide) lengthwise strips and join to top and bottom of quilt. Cut 2 more (15½″-wide) lengthwise strips and join to sides of quilt.

6. By hand or machine, outline-quilt block pieces. Quilt borders with diagonal lines as shown.

7. Bind with muslin. (See Binding Your Quilt, page 89.)

Lincoln's Platform

You'll need no templates for this traditional quilt pattern, sometimes called Churn Dash or Monkey Wrench. All the pieces can be cut using rotary-cutting equipment.

Lincoln's Platform Quilting Pattern

Half Pattern

Trace pattern. Lift tracing paper. Reverse at dots and trace other half.

Finished Sizes

Quilt: $67\frac{2}{3}''$ x $78\frac{1}{4}''$
Blocks: 42 $(7\frac{1}{2}'')$ Blocks

Fabrics

Muslin	4 yards
Assorted solids	$2\frac{5}{8}$ yards*
Backing	5 yards
Muslin for binding	1 yard

*$\frac{1}{8}$ yard will yield pieces for 2 blocks.

Instructions

1. From muslin, cut 2 $(2\frac{1}{2}''$ x $80'')$ and 2 $(2\frac{1}{2}''$ x $70'')$ border strips and set aside.

From remaining muslin, cut 30 $(8'')$ setting squares, 11 $(8\frac{3}{8}'')$ squares, 1 $(8\frac{3}{4}'')$ square, 84 $(3\frac{7}{8}'')$ squares, and 168 $(2'')$ squares (piece A). (See Block Assembly diagram on next page.)

Cut each of the 11 $(8\frac{3}{8}'')$ muslin squares in half diagonally to make 22 half-square side triangles. (See Making Half-Square and Quarter-Square Triangles, page 5.) Cut the $8\frac{3}{4}''$ square into quarters diagonally to make 4 quarter-square corner triangles. Cut the 84 $(3\frac{7}{8}'')$ squares in half diagonally to make 168 half-square triangles (piece B).

From assorted solids, cut 84 $(3\frac{7}{8}'')$ squares (2 of same color for each block) and 210 $(2'')$ piece C squares (5 of same color for each block). Cut the 84 $(3\frac{7}{8}'')$ squares in half diagonally to make a total of 168 half-square triangles (piece D).

2. Follow Block Assembly diagram to make 42 Lincoln's Platform blocks.

3. Follow Quilt Top Assembly diagram on next page to join blocks with setting squares, side triangles, and corner triangles.

4. Join the 2 $(2\frac{1}{2}''$ x $70'')$ border strips to top and bottom of quilt. Trim to match edges of quilt. Join the $(2\frac{1}{2}''$ x $80'')$ border strips to sides of quilt. Trim to match edges of quilt.

5. By hand or machine, outline-quilt muslin pieces A and B. Transfer quilting pattern at left to setting squares and quilt.

6. Bind quilt with bias binding made from muslin. (See Binding Your Quilt, page 89.)

Block Assembly

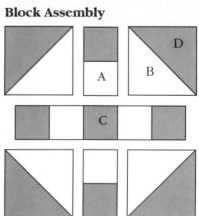

Lincoln's Platform Block

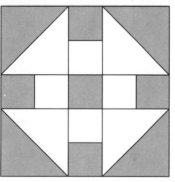

Quilt Top Assembly

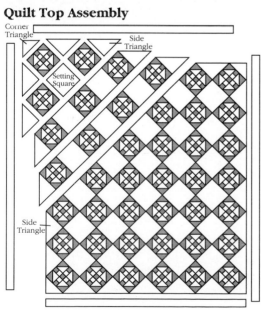

Finished Sizes
Quilt: 75″ x 85″
Blocks: 412 (3″ x 5″) Bricks
26 (2½″ x 3″) Half Bricks

Fabrics
Assorted dk. and lt. scraps*
Backing   5½ yards
*⅛ yard of fabric will yield 7 bricks.

Instructions
1. Cut 206 dk. and 206 lt. (3½″ x 5½″) rectangles (bricks). Cut 13 dk. and 13 lt. (2¾″ x 3½″) rectangles (half bricks).

2. Following Quilt Top Assembly diagram for dk. and lt. placement, join 16 bricks and 2 half-bricks to make Row A. Join 17 bricks to make Row B. Continue to follow diagram to make Row C and Row D. Continue joining bricks and half bricks to make a total of 7 Row As, 6 Row Bs, 6 Row Cs, and 6 Row Ds. Join vertical rows as shown in diagram.

3. Prepare backing to extend 2½″ beyond edges of quilt top. Quilt an X in each brick and each half brick (see photograph). Fold backing to front of quilt to form 1″ self binding, turn under raw edge ¼″, and slipstitch to quilt top.

was ... nche
Fleming Harwood ... used a postcard for her template, the fashionable thing for young quilters to do at the turn of the century. Barbara Harwood, Blanche's daughter-in-law, is now the owner of this quilt, whose pattern is also known as Brick Wall.

You can duplicate Blanche's technique by using a standard postcard as a template. Or use your rotary-cutting equipment for a faster job.

Quilt Top Assembly

Row A
Row B
Row C
Row D

Half Brick
Brick

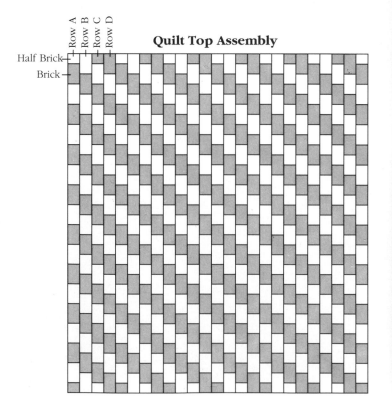

This design is an especially good choice for a beginning quilter. Cutting, piecing, and quilting are all simple and straightforward.

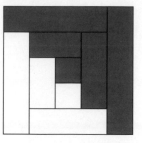

Block 1

Shadow and Light

Hand-dyed fabric is the secret to the beauty of this striking wall quilt. Seven or eight graduated shades of each color were used in the quilt in the photograph. Ready-dyed fabric can be substituted; but if you'd like to use the real thing, see page 160 to find out where to order hand-dyed fabric in graduated shades.

Finished Sizes
Quilt: 49¾″ x 61¾″
Blocks: 49 (6¼″) Sampler Blocks

Fabrics

Assorted reds	½ yard
Assorted browns	½ yard
Assorted purples	½ yard
Assorted roses	½ yard
Assorted lavenders	½ yard
Assorted rusts	½ yard
Assorted blues	½ yard
Muslin	1⅞ yards
Backing	3¾ yards
Muslin for binding	¾ yard

Instructions

1. To make Block 1, cut red fabrics into 1¾″-wide crosswise strips. Machine-piece strips, log-cabin fashion, into 7 blocks. (See Block 1 diagram.) If you aren't familiar with log-cabin piecing, refer to Block Assembly diagram on page 18.

2. To make Block 2, cut brown fabrics into 14 (4″) squares, 7 (4⅜″) squares, and 7 (3⅝″) squares (piece C). Cut 4″ squares in half diagonally to make 28 half-square triangles (piece A). (See Making Half-Square and Quarter-Square Triangles, page 5.) Cut 4⅜″ squares into quarters diagonally to form 28 quarter-square triangles (piece B).

Follow Block 2 diagram to make 7 blocks, first joining Bs to center square C, then adding As.

3. To make Block 3, cut purple fabrics into 2⅝″-wide strips. Cut strips into 2⅝″ squares. Follow block diagrams to make 4 Block 3As and 3 Block 3Bs.

4. To make Block 4, cut pieces from rose fabrics as indicated on templates on page 135. Refer to Block 4 diagram and photograph to make 1

Block 2

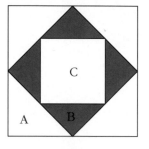

Block 3A

Block 3B

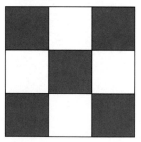

Graduated shades of seven solid colors combine with muslin to form a graphic patchwork statement. This sampler quilt uses many quick-piecing techniques.

block as follows: Join 1 A to 1 B along curve. (Unless you are extremely proficient at machine-piecing curves, these blocks are best pieced by hand.) Join 1 reversed A to 1 reversed B along curve. Now join 1 C to 1 D and 1 reversed C to 1 reversed D along curves. Join the 4 squares to form block as shown in diagram. Repeat for 6 more blocks.

5. To make Block 5, make a triangle template by cutting a 7⅛″ square in half diagonally. Use template to cut 7 triangles from several shades of lavender. Cut remainder of lavender fabric into 1½″-wide strips. Join strips along long edges. Use template to cut 7 strip-pieced triangles. (See Cutting Strip-Pieced Triangle diagram below.) Join solid triangles with strip-pieced triangles as shown in Block 5 diagram to make 7 blocks.

6. To make Block 6, cut rust fabrics into 28 (2¾″) squares (piece A) and 14 (4″) squares. Cut the 4″ squares into 28 half-square triangles (piece B). Follow Block 6 diagram and photograph to make 7 blocks, first joining A squares to form 4-patch unit and then adding B triangles to 4-patch unit.

7. To make Block 7, cut blue fabrics into 28 (4″) squares. Cut squares into 56 half-square triangles. Follow Block 7 diagram to make 1 block as follows: Join 1 light triangle and 1 dark triangle along long edge. Working with same 2 shades of blue, repeat 3 more times to make 4 squares. Join squares to make block. Repeat for 6 more blocks.

8. Join each set of blocks into a 7-block horizontal row as shown.

9. From muslin, cut 6 (2½″ x 44″) sashing strips. Join rows with sashing strips.

10. From muslin, cut 2 (3½″-wide) borders and join to top and bottom of quilt. Cut 2 (3½″-wide) borders and join to sides of quilt.

11. Machine- or hand-quilt in-the-ditch of all seams. Bind with bias binding made from muslin. (See Binding Your Quilt, page 89.)

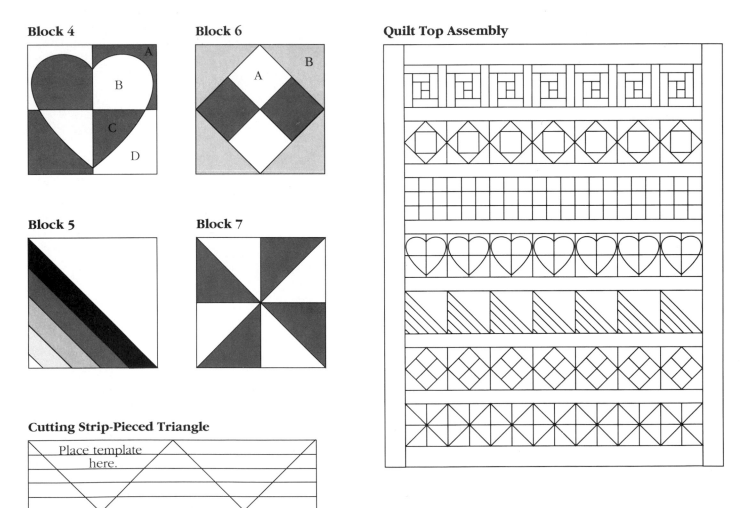

Block 4

Block 6

Quilt Top Assembly

Block 5

Block 7

Cutting Strip-Pieced Triangle

Place template here.

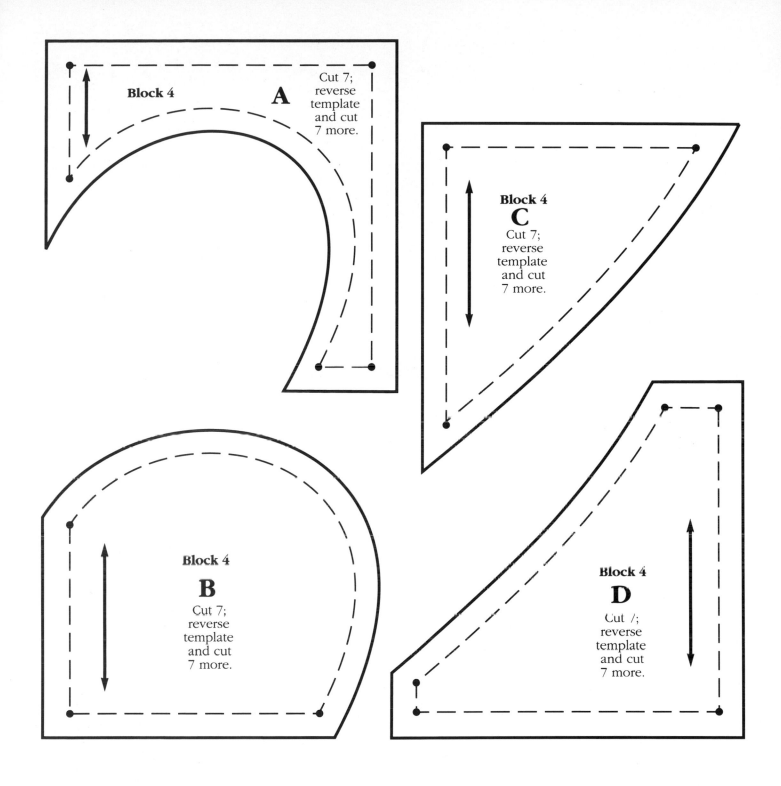

Block 4

A

Cut 7; reverse template and cut 7 more.

Block 4

C

Cut 7; reverse template and cut 7 more.

Block 4

B

Cut 7; reverse template and cut 7 more.

Block 4

D

Cut 7; reverse template and cut 7 more.

Double
Wedding Ring

This version of the quilted classic shortens cutting and piecing time by incorporating the six or more tiny pieces that usually make up the arc (piece B) into one large piece.

The Double Wedding Ring is one of the most loved of all quilt designs–and one of the most time-consuming to piece. This adaptation cuts piecing time in half.

Finished Size
Quilt: 90⅜″ x 114⅝″

Fabrics
Muslin	8½ yards
Blue print	7½ yards
Red print	¾ yard
Rose print	¾ yard
Backing	6½ yards
Muslin for binding	1 yard

Instructions

1. Cut pieces as indicated on templates on pages 138 and 139.

2. Follow Ring Assembly diagram to make 32 whole rings as shown in Diagram 1. (See instructions for sewing curves, page 8.) Follow shaded section only of Ring Assembly diagram to make 6 quarter rings as shown in Diagram 2 and 8 quarter rings as shown in Diagram 3. (*Note:* You will have 17 piece As remaining.)

3. Following Quilt Top Assembly diagram on page 138 for placement, join whole rings, quarter rings, and remaining piece As.

4. Either by hand or machine, quilt in-the-ditch around arcs. Transfer quilting pattern on page 140 to muslin centers (piece As) and quilt.

5. Bind with continuous bias binding made from muslin. (See Binding Your Quilt, page 89.)

Ring Assembly

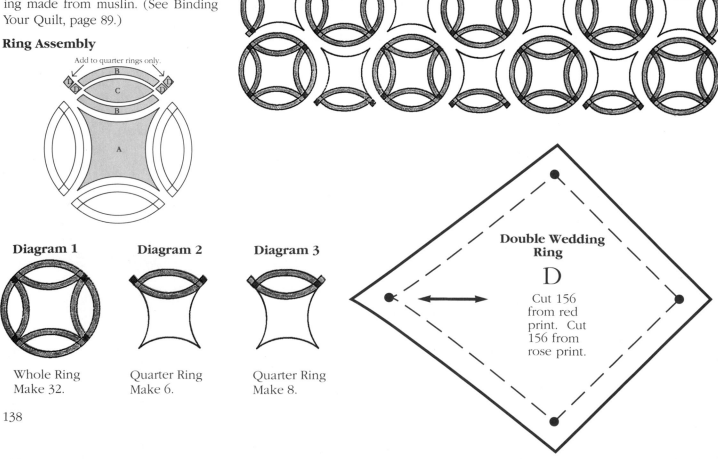

Add to quarter rings only.

B
C
B
A

Quilt Top Assembly

Diagram 1

Whole Ring
Make 32.

Diagram 2

Quarter Ring
Make 6.

Diagram 3

Quarter Ring
Make 8.

Double Wedding Ring

D

Cut 156 from red print. Cut 156 from rose print.

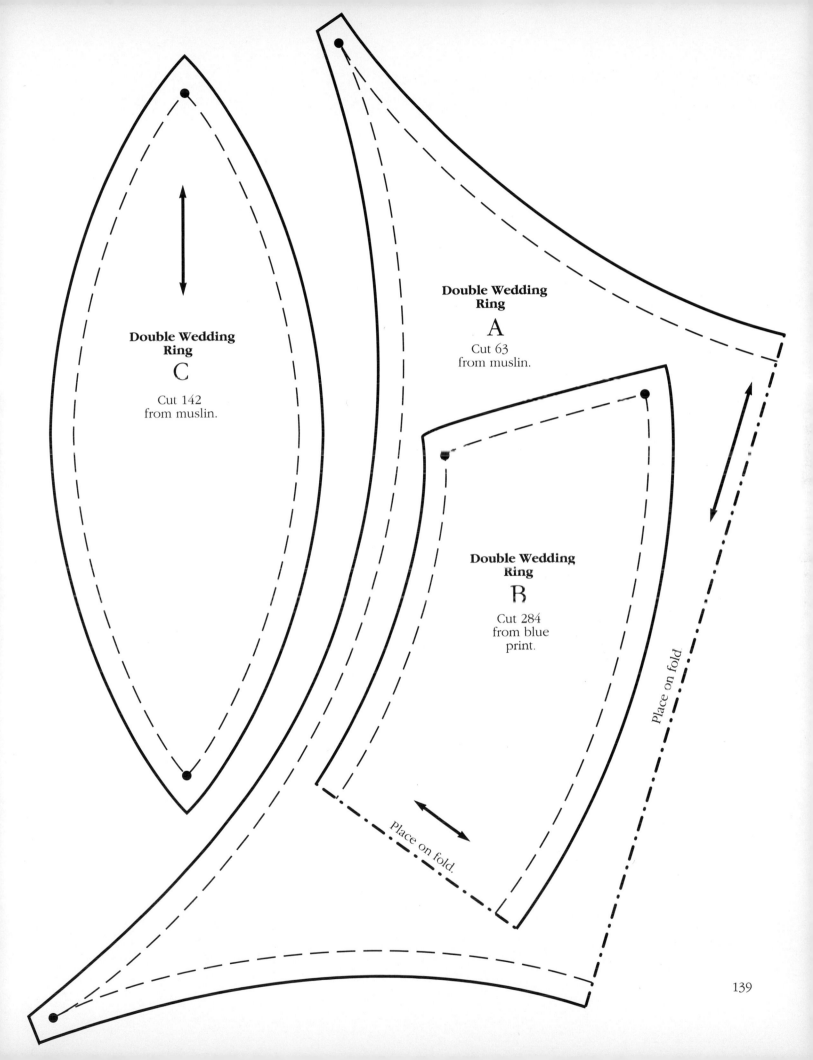

Double Wedding Ring

C

Cut 142
from muslin.

Double Wedding Ring

A

Cut 63
from muslin.

Double Wedding Ring

B

Cut 284
from blue
print.

Place on fold

Place on fold.

139

Double Wedding Ring Quilting Pattern

Snowball and Nine Patch

This quilt, which was made by Nancy Nichols Butler around 1930, is an example of a two-block design. (*Double Irish Chain*, page 109, is another.) A two-block quilt is made up of two simple square block designs, each of which usually has a separate historic name. The blocks are joined in an alternating fashion to make a more elaborate overall pattern. The two blocks that make up this quilt can be pieced by machine.

Finished Sizes
Quilt: 88" x 89"
Blocks: 42 (8¼") Nine-Patch Blocks
       30 (8¼") Snowball Blocks
       12 Half-Snowball Blocks
       4 Quarter-Snowball Blocks

Fabrics
Assorted lt. prints	2⅜ yards
Assorted dk. prints	2⅛ yards
Green solid	3 yards
Red solid	1 yard
Dk. green solid for border	2⅝ yards
Backing	5½ yards

Instructions

1. To make large triangles, cut 5 (9½") squares from light print. Cut squares in half diagonally to make 10 half-square triangles. (See Making Half-Square and Quarter-Square Triangles, page 5.) Set aside.

2. To make Nine-Patch blocks, cut dark print and remaining light print into (3¼"-wide) crosswise strips. Follow Nine-Patch Construction diagram, page 12, to piece 4 dark/light/dark bands as shown in Figure 1 and 7 light/dark/light bands as shown in Figure 2. Cut across bands to make pieced strips as shown in Figure 3 (except make strips 3¼"-wide, instead of 2" as diagram indicates). Following Figures 4 and 5, join pieced strips to make 42 Nine-Patch blocks.

3. Using templates at right, cut 30 octagons, 12 half octagons, and 4 quarter octagons from green solid.

To make triangle As, cut 11 (2⅞"-wide) crosswise strips from red solid. Cut strips into 2⅞" squares. Cut squares in half diagonally to make 132 half-square triangles.

To make triangle Bs, cut 1 (3⅜") crosswise strip from red solid. Cut strip into 3⅜" squares. Cut squares into quarters diagonally to make 32 quarter-square triangles.

4. Follow Snowball Block diagram to make 30 Snowball blocks. Follow Half-Snowball Block diagram to make 12 Half-Snowball blocks. Follow Quarter-Snowball Block diagram to make 4 Quarter-Snowball blocks.

5. Follow the Quilt Top Assembly diagram to join all blocks, half blocks,

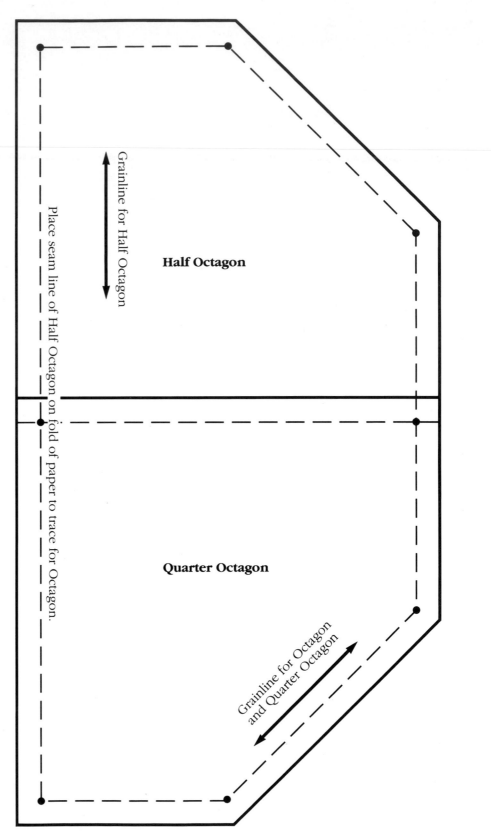

quarter blocks, and large triangles.

6. Cut 2 (3½"-wide) border strips from dark green solid and join to sides of quilt. Cut 2 (3½"-wide) border strips from dark green solid and join to top and bottom of quilt.

7. Quilt as desired. Fold ¾" of the border to back of quilt. Turn under ¼" seam allowance and slipstitch to quilt back to form self binding.

Nine-Patch Block

Half-Snowball Block

B   A

Half
Octagon

B

Snowball Block

A

Octagon

Quarter-Snowball Block

B

Quarter
Octagon

B

Quilt Top Assembly

Quarter
Snowball

Half
Snowball

Large
Triangle

Snug-and-Warm Stadium Quilt

If you're looking for something creative to do with those old jeans and cords your children have outgrown, here's a great idea. Cut them up and make them into a quilt to keep out the chilly autumn breezes at football games.

Vonda Roberts, mother of three teenagers, used ten pairs of worn denim and corduroy pants to make this quilt. If you don't have enough old pants to make a quilt, look around at yard sales and thrift stores to add to your supply.

No batting is used in this quilt, since the top and backing are made from heavy fabric.

Finished Sizes
Quilt: 57" x 75"
Blocks: 18 (9") Block As
17 (9") Block Bs

Fabrics and Materials
Worn denim and corduroy scraps
Backing*   4¾ yards
Baby or sports yarn:
  dk. blue, lt. blue   1 skein each
Yarn needle
*Use heavy fabric such as denim or corduroy for backing. Or piece backing from additional denim and corduroy scraps.

Instructions

1. Cut denim and corduroy scraps into 162 (3½") squares and 51 (3½" x 9½") rectangles.

2. Follow block diagrams and photograph to join squares to make 18 Block As. Join rectangles to make 17 Block Bs.

3. Follow Quilt Top Assembly diagram to join blocks in 7 horizontal rows of 5 blocks each, alternating Block As and Block Bs as shown. Join rows.

4. Cut enough 3½"-wide denim strips to piece inner and outer borders and join to quilt as shown in Quilt Top Assembly diagram.

5. Prepare backing to match quilt top measurements. With right sides facing and raw edges aligned, join top to backing, leaving an opening at bottom large enough for turning. Turn quilt through opening. Slipstitch opening closed.

6. Cut yarn into 12" lengths. For each tie, thread yarn needle with 1 length each of dk. blue and lt. blue yarn. Tie quilt at regular intervals through both layers.

Block A

Block B

Quilt Top Assembly

Kids and grown-ups will enjoy cheering their team to victory wrapped in this quilt, made from denim and corduroy scraps. It's also a handy accessory for picnics and outdoor concerts.

CHAPTER SEVEN

• • •

Through the medium of quilts, each generation passes on to the next a little of itself. Just as was true with my sisters and me, our children can trace their childhood memories on the tops of handmade quilts—many made especially for them.

When my daughter was five or six, Mama made for her a Sunbonnet Sue quilt from scraps left over from her little girl dresses. For my son, she made a Lemoyne Star from brown prints. My sister made an appliquéd butterfly quilt in softest pink for her baby daughter. And I made a quilt for my children that had a head, legs, and arms attached, making it a giant rag doll.

The list of all the quilts we've made for the little ones over the years goes on and on. But the one that is freshest in my mind, the one that is quilted totally from heart strings, is the one I made this Christmas for my grandson, now a member of the Terrible Twos. Under flaps sewn into its squares hide birds, elephants, bears, pigs, and other animals. He likes to uncover each animal in turn and repeat its name or the sound that it makes. The quilt serves him threefold: as a cover, a toy, and a learning tool.

When he is older, I trust my grandson will appreciate the myriad elements that are sewn into that quilt and all the others made by the women of his family. Whether scrap-bag splashes of color, patchwork playhouse wonderlands, or rough woolen covers, quilts are much more than combinations of fabric, batting, and thread. Hidden within the folds of each quilt is the heritage of someone's memories of happiness, sorrow, pride, necessity, fellowship, love. Where else could one find his family history so beautifully—and comfortably—preserved?

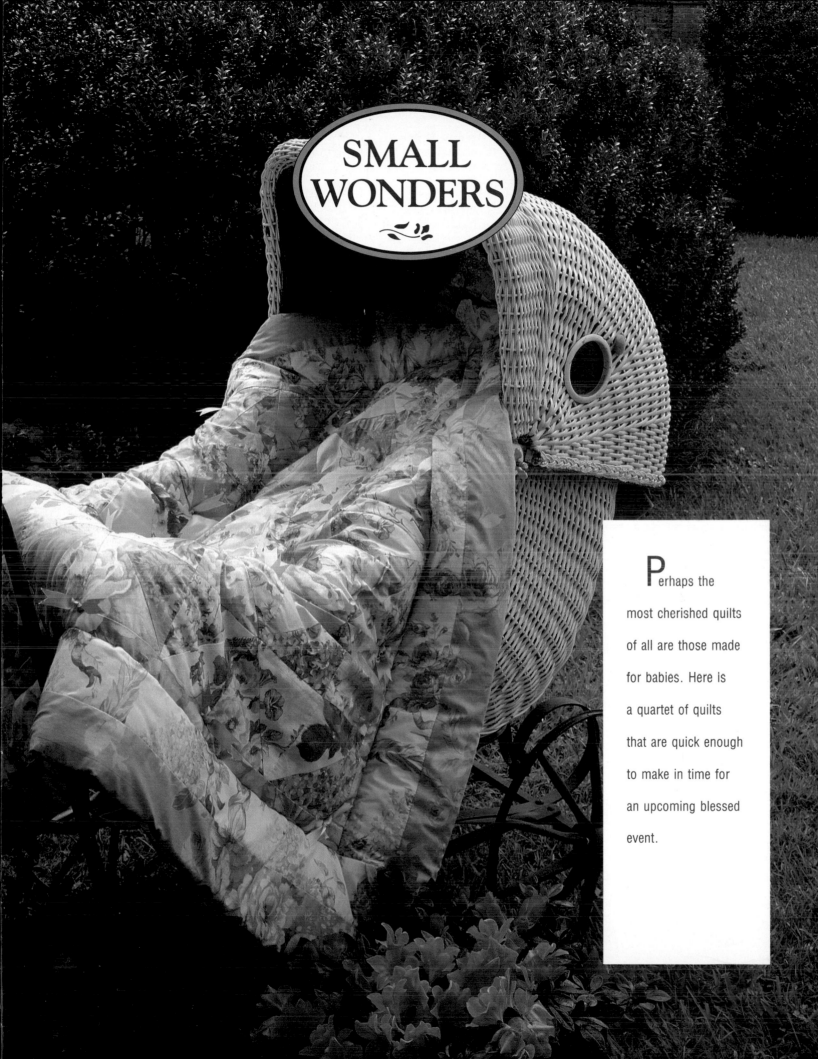

SMALL WONDERS

Perhaps the most cherished quilts of all are those made for babies. Here is a quartet of quilts that are quick enough to make in time for an upcoming blessed event.

Country Garden Crib Quilt

Flowered chintz combines with the quick-piece triangle method for a quick-and-easy quilt that's sweet enough for the treasure it's meant to wrap.

Finished Sizes
Quilt: 44" x 54"
Blocks: 12 (10") Blocks

Fabrics and Materials

Lt. floral chintz	¾ yard
Dk. floral chintz	¾ yard
Lt. chintz for borders	1¼ yards
Dk. chintz for borders	1⅜ yards
Backing	1⅝ yards

3½ yards (⅜"-wide) satin ribbon in assorted colors
Yarn needle

Instructions

1. Refer to Quick-Piece Triangle Method diagram on page 32 to make pieced squares as follows: With right sides facing and raw edges aligned, place lt. floral chintz on top of dk. floral chintz. Use Quick-Piece Triangle Template on page 34 to trace 48 triangles onto fabric as shown in Figure 1. Machine-stitch ¼" on either side of drawn diagonal lines as shown in Figure 2. Cut apart along drawn horizontal and vertical lines as shown in Figure 3 to form 2-layer squares. Cut squares apart along drawn diagonal lines between the lines of stitching to form 2-layer triangles as indicated in Figures 4 and 5. Unfold triangle and press seam to 1 side to form square as shown in Figure 6. Repeat to make 48 pieced squares.

2. Follow Country Garden Block diagram to join 4 pieced squares to form 1 block. Repeat to make 12 blocks.

3. Follow Quilt Top Assembly diagram to join blocks in 4 horizontal rows of 3 blocks each. Join rows.

4. Cut 4 (1½"-wide) border strips from dk. chintz and join to quilt as shown in diagram. Cut 4 (3½"-wide) border strips from lt. chintz and join to quilt. Cut 4 (3½"-wide) border strips from dk. chintz and join to quilt.

5. Layer batting; top, right side up; and backing, right side down. With batting against feed dogs, join layers along sides and bottom. Turn through opening, with batting on inside. Slip-stitch opening closed.

6. Cut ribbon into 20 (6") pieces. Beginning at center of quilt, tie bows at all block corners as follows: Thread yarn needle with 1 (6") length of ribbon. Sew ribbon through all thicknesses and tie on top (see photograph). Machine-quilt in-the-ditch between borders.

Country Garden Block **Quilt Top Assembly**

The romance of old-fashioned chintz brings the warmth of a summer day to a sweet little girl any time of the year.

Calico Strings

The pieced print panels that highlight this nursery quilt are made using string piecing and the quilt-as-you-piece method. Choose prints from your scrap bag, or purchase coordinating fabrics in the color scheme of your choice to make this sturdy quick quilt that's designed to last for generations.

Finished Size
Quilt: 36" x 44½"

Fabrics
Blue print for sashing, borders, backing, and binding	3⅛ yards
Assorted prints	1¼ yards

Instructions

1. From blue print, cut 4 (6½" x 39") backing panels, 6 (2½" x 39") sashing strips, and 8 (3½" x 39") border strips.

2. Cut assorted prints into crosswise strings of varying widths, ranging from 1¾" to 2¾".

3. From batting, cut 4 (6½" x 39") rectangles, 3 (2½" x 39") rectangles, and 4 (3½" x 39") rectangles.

4. Baste 1 (6½" x 39") batting panel to wrong side of 1 (6½" x 39") backing panel. Following String-Pieced Panels diagram below, lay 1 print string, right side up, diagonally across top right corner of batting. Trim and add excess to remaining strings. With right sides facing and raw edges aligned, lay second string on top of first. Trim and reserve excess as before. Join through all layers as shown in Figure 1. Flip String 2 over and finger-press as shown in Figure 2. Lay a third string on top of String 2 and join as before. Continue to add strings in this manner until entire panel is covered. Trim strings even with backing panel. Repeat to make 1 more string-pieced panel.

String-Pieced Panels

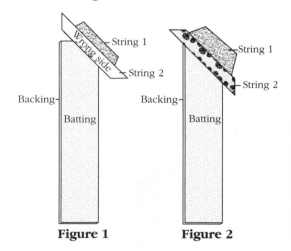

Figure 1   **Figure 2**

Repeat Step 4 to make 2 more panels, this time beginning string piecing in top left corner, for a total of 4 panels.

5. Refer to Quilt-As-You-Piece diagram below to attach 1 sashing strip to 1 string-pieced panel as follows: With raw edges aligned, layer back sashing strip, wrong side down; string-pieced panel, backing side down; front sashing strip, right side down; and 1 (2½″ x 39″) piece of batting. Baste all layers together. With batting against feed dogs, stitch along the seam line as indicated. Trim the batting from the seam allowance.

Fold sashing strips and batting outward. Topstitch ¼″ from seam line on top sashing strip. (See Quilt Assembly diagram below.)

Join next string-pieced panel in same manner. Topstitch ¼″ from seam line on top sashing strip as indicated in Quilt Assembly diagram.

Join remaining sashing strips and string-pieced panels in same manner.

6. Trim 4 of the 3½″ x 39″ border strips and 2 of the 3½″ x 39″ batting strips to match sides of quilt and join to sides of quilt using quilt-as-you-piece method. Trim remaining border and batting strips and join to top and bottom of quilt using quilt-as-you-piece method. Topstitch ¼″ from edge of string-pieced panels on border all around quilt. (See Quilt Assembly diagram.)

7. Round off corners of quilt, using small plate or French curve. Bind with bias binding made from remaining blue print. (See Binding Your Quilt, page 89.)

Quilt-As-You-Piece

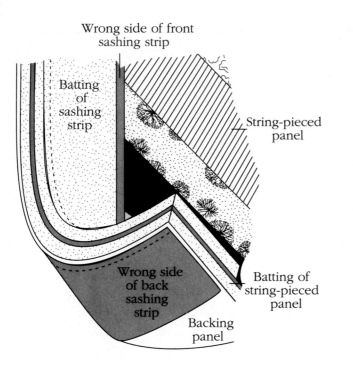

Wrong side of front sashing strip

Batting of sashing strip

String-pieced panel

Wrong side of back sashing strip

Batting of string-pieced panel

Backing panel

Quilt Assembly

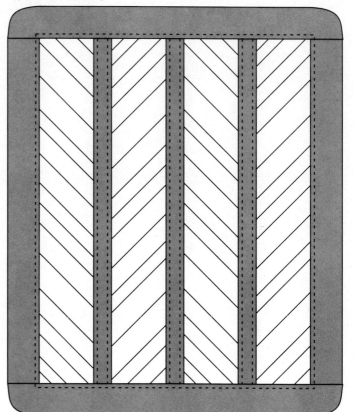

Satin and Bows

Gather all your pretty print scraps, add some pastel satin and ribbons, and quick-piece a crib set that will please any new mother. From a collection of small squares, you can make a crib quilt, bumper pad, and a warm bunting to wrap around the newborn.

CRIB QUILT

Finished Size
Quilt: 39″ x 48″
Blocks: 12 (9″) Nine-Patch Blocks

Fabrics and Materials
Assorted print scraps
Assorted polyester satin scraps
White polyester
    satin for border   1⅛ yards
Print for border   1¼ yards
Backing   1½ yards
7 yards (⅜′-wide) satin ribbon in
    assorted colors
Yarn needle

Instructions

1. From assorted print and satin scraps, cut 108 (3½″) squares.

2. Join squares randomly to make 12 Nine-Patch blocks. (See Quilt Top Assembly diagram below.)

3. Follow Quilt Top Assembly diagram to join blocks in 4 horizontal rows of 3 blocks each. Join rows.

4. Cut 4 (3½″-wide) border strips from white satin and join to quilt. Cut 4 (3½″-wide) border strips from print and join to quilt.

5. Layer batting; top, right side up; and backing, right side down. With batting against feed dogs, join layers along sides and bottom. Turn through opening, with batting on inside. Slip-stitch opening closed.

6. Cut ribbon into 20 (12″) pieces. Beginning at center of quilt, tie bows at all block corners as follows: Thread yarn needle with 1 (12″) length of ribbon. Sew ribbon through all thicknesses and tie bow on top (see photograph). Machine-quilt in-the-ditch between print and satin borders.

Bumper Pad Assembly

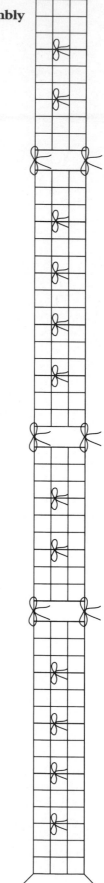

Quilt Top Assembly

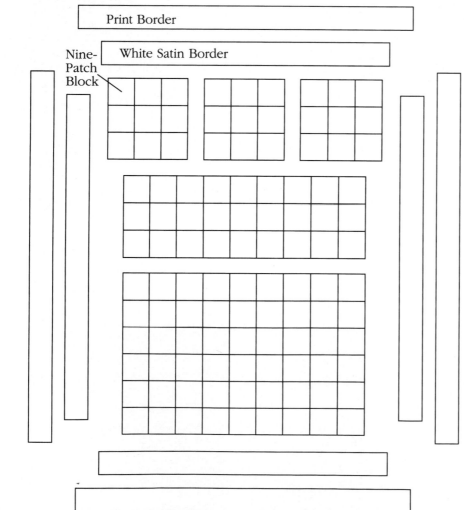

Print Border

White Satin Border

Nine-Patch Block

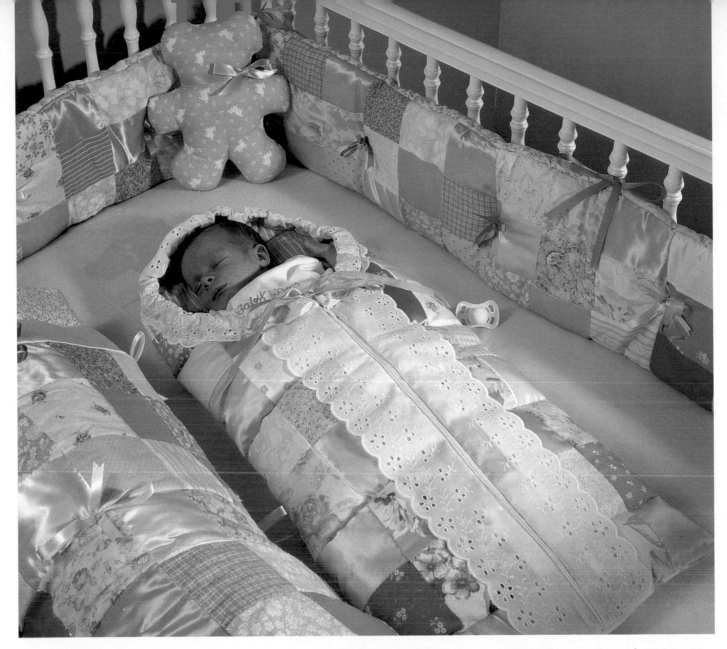

BUMPER PAD

Finished Size
Blocks: 16 (9″) Nine-Patch Blocks

Fabrics and Materials
Assorted print scraps*
Assorted polyester satin scraps*
Backing   1⅜ yards
Extra-loft batting
16½ yards (⅜″-wide) satin ribbon in
    assorted colors
Yarn needle
*⅛ yard will yield 12 squares.

Instructions
1. Cut assorted print and satin scraps into 144 (3½″) squares.
2. Join squares randomly to make 16 Nine-Patch blocks. (See Quilt Top Assembly diagram, page 154.)

3. Join Nine-Patch blocks in 2 rows of 5 blocks each and 2 rows of 3 blocks each (see Bumper Pad Assembly diagram).
4. Cut backing fabric into 2 (9½″ x 45½″) and 2 (9½″ x 27½″) panels. Cut batting into 4 (9½″ x 45½″) and 4 (9½″ x 27½″) panels.
5. Layer 2 (9½″ x 45½″) batting panels; 1 row of 5 Nine-Patch blocks, right side up; and 1 (9½″ x 45½″) backing panel, right side down. With batting against feed dogs, join layers along 3 sides, leaving 1 end open for turning. Turn through opening, with batting on inside. Slipstitch opening closed.
Repeat Step 5 to make 1 more 9″ x 45″ pad.
6. Repeat Step 5, using remaining

Nine-Patch rows, batting, and backing panels, to make 2 (9″ x 27″) pads.
7. Cut ribbon into 16 (28″) lengths and 12 (12″) lengths.
8. Lay pads side by side as shown in Bumper Pad Assembly diagram. Thread yarn needle with 1 (28″) length of ribbon. Sew ribbon through all layers at the tip of 1 corner of 1 pad. Tie ribbon in a knot, leaving 2 long tails. Repeat to tie remaining 28″ lengths of ribbon at all corners of all pads. Tie pads together as indicated.
Thread needle with 1 (12″) length of ribbon. Sew ribbon through all layers at center of seam line where 2 blocks are joined (see photograph and diagram). Tie ribbon in a bow on top. Repeat at center of each seam line where 2 blocks join.

This patchwork baby bunting is easy to make; and all the materials, including the polyester satin, are machine washable. The same goes for the materials in the crib quilt and bumper pad.

BUNTING

Fabric and Materials
Assorted print scraps*
Assorted polyester satin scraps*
Lining   1 yard
Extra-loft batting
2½ yards (3″-wide) flat eyelet lace
1¾ yards (⅜″-wide) satin ribbon
18″ zipper
*⅛ yard will yield 12 squares.

Instructions
1. Cut assorted scraps into 98 (3½″) squares. Join squares as shown in Bunting Pattern Placement diagram on page 157.

2. Enlarge Bunting Pattern. (See Enlarging Patterns, page 35.) Place pattern on pieced square unit as shown in Bunting Pattern Placement diagram. Cut out, adding ½″ seam allowance. Cut 1 bunting shape from lining fabric, adding ½″ seam allowance. Cut 2 bunting shapes from batting, adding ½″ seam allowance.

3. Layer lining, right side down; batting; and bunting top, right side up. Machine-quilt in-the-ditch along seam lines of each 4-square unit. Trim batting from seam allowance. Zigzag raw edges around bunting.

4. Cut 2 (19″) pieces and 1 (42″) piece of eyelet lace.

5. With raw edges aligned, baste 1 (19″) piece of lace to each center front edge on right side of pieced bunting top.

6. Turn under raw edges along center front of bunting ½″ and baste. Following manufacturer's instructions, insert zipper in front of bunting.

7. With right sides facing, raw edges aligned, and zipper centered at front of bunting, join bottom edges with ½″ seam. Stitch again ¼″ from edge to reinforce seam. Turn bunting right side out.

8. Turn under ½″ at each end of 42″ piece of eyelet lace and baste. With right side of lace facing bunting lining and raw edges aligned, stitch lace around hood of bunting. Turn lace to right side of bunting and stitch in place 1½″ from edge of hood to bind raw edges and to form casing.

9. Insert satin ribbon in casing.

Bunting Pattern
1 square=1".
Enlarge 400%.

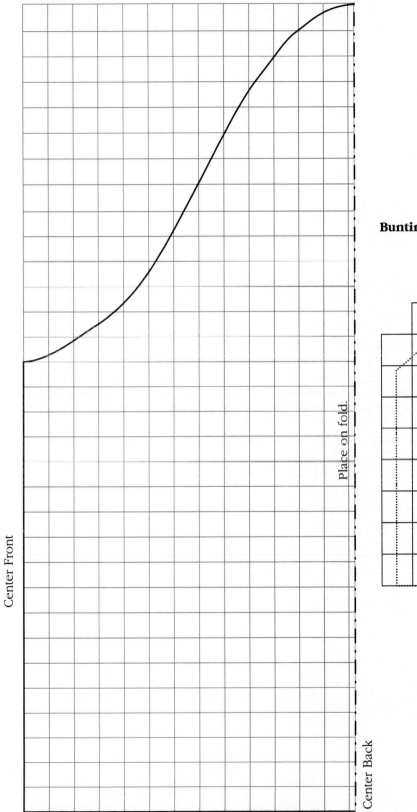

Center Front

Place on fold.

Center Back

Bunting Pattern Placement

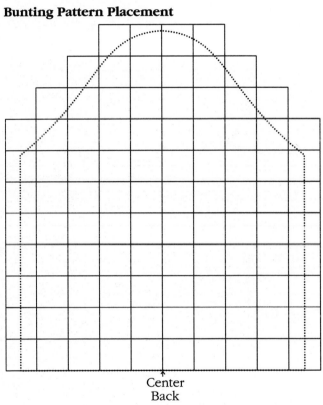

Center
Back

157

Antique Cradle Cover

This little coverlet, circa 1880, shows that the sewing machine was used for quilting more than 100 years ago.

Finished Sizes
Quilt: 16½" x 31⅞"
Blocks: 20 (4½") Nine-Patch Blocks

Fabrics

Red print	½ yard
Assorted lt. prints	⅜ yard
Assorted dk. prints	¼ yard
Backing	2¼ yards
Red print for binding	½ yard

Instructions

1. From red print, cut 12 (5") setting squares, 7 (5⅜") squares, and 1 (5¾") square. Cut 5⅜" squares in half diagonally to make 14 half-square triangles. (See Making Half-Square and Quarter-Square Triangles, page 5.) Set aside for use as large triangles. Cut 5¾" square into quarters diagonally to make 4 quarter-square triangles. Set aside for use as small triangles.

2. To make Nine-Patch blocks, cut assorted prints into 2"-wide crosswise strips. Follow Nine-Patch Construction diagram on page 12 to piece 2 light/dark/light bands as shown in Figure 2 and 1 dark/light/dark band as shown in Figure 1. Cut across bands at 2" intervals to make pieced strips as shown in Figure 3. Follow Figures 4 and 5 to join pieced strips to make 20 Nine-Patch blocks.

3. Follow Quilt Top Assembly diagram to set Nine-Patch blocks together with setting squares, large triangles, and small triangles.

4. Machine-quilt with straight lines as shown in photograph. Bind with bias binding made from red print. (See Binding Your Quilt, page 89.)

Quilt Top Assembly

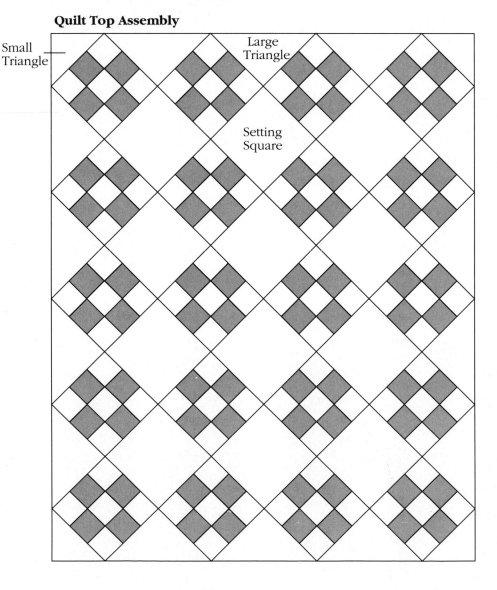